1. Friendship as Sacrament

Friendship
as
Sacrament

Friendship
as
Sacrament

by

Carmen L. Caltagirone

ALBA · HOUSE   NEW · YORK

SOCIETY OF ST. PAUL, 2187 VICTORY BLVD., STATEN ISLAND, NEW YORK 10314

Library of Congress Cataloging-in-Publication Data

Caltagirone, Carmen L.
  Friendship as Sacrament.

  Bibliography: p.
  1. Friendship—Religious aspects—Christianity.
  2. Love—Religious aspects—Christianity. 3. Interpersonal relations—Religious aspects—Christianity.
  4. Spiritual life—Catholic authors. I. Title.
  BV4647.F7C35   1988   241'.676   88-3404
  ISBN 0-8189-0532-8

Designed, printed and bound in the United States of
America by the Fathers and Brothers of the
Society of St. Paul, 2187 Victory Boulevard,
Staten Island, New York 10314, as part of their
communications apostolate.

Printing Information:

Current Printing - first digit   1   2   3   4   5   6   7   8   9   10   11   12   13   14   15   16   17   18   19   20

Year of Current Printing - first year shown
          1988   1989   1990   1991   1992   1993   1994   1995   1996   1997   1998   1999   2000   2001   2002

To
Sister Ann Regan, S.N.J.M.
who is a surprise gift to me
from God and whose passion for God
has renewed my own.

AUTHOR'S NOTE

A great effort has been made throughout this manuscript to avoid sexist language wherever possible. However, all quotations from Scripture and other literary sources appear just as they do in the copyright versions. Also, I chose not to use inclusive language devices when referring to God, finding that they were very awkward and generally broke the flow.

Preface

THERE WAS a point in my life when I realized in a profound way that we are meant to seek the face of God in every face we meet. This little book is a reflection on the agonies and ecstasies of that search. It deals mostly with love and friendship. It explores the concept of friendship as sacrament, discussing how our deeply personal relationships are meant to be at once a sign and affirmation of God's boundless, constant love.

For over 18 years, the great privilege of devoting my life to work within the Church has afforded me countless opportunities to experience the wondrous magic of people. I have shared in the pain and confusion, healing and growth of many children and adults. I have witnessed the astounding transformations that result when two or more people bond together in intimacy. I have been especially overwhelmed by the uplifting transformations that result when the power of God is recognized in a relationship.

My intention in writing this book is that those who read it will be excited by the wonder of a God who comes to them in the tender love of another. It is my hope that the recognition of this wonder will lead to a deeper intimacy with the God of love and a more profound understanding of human relationships. To inspire in the reader a renewed passion for God, for others and for all of life is my greatest desire.

This book does not pretend to be a theological treatise or a psychological essay; it is a personal reflection on the vitality of our relatedness to divine and human persons. I do not pretend to know the intricacies of human love; I write out of the lived experience of a God whose face I have sought and found in the faces of those who have offered love on his behalf.

We often think only of our parents as those persons who "hand on life" to us. All those who have shared their personal journey to God with me and with whom I have shared mine, have handed on life to me. These people have played a significant role in the formulating of the thoughts presented here. I am grateful to them, not just for their contribution to this book, but also and especially for the way they have enriched my life.

There is the obvious debt of gratitude I owe to my parents, Joe and Mary Jane, who first taught me the meaning of love. In writing a book dealing with relationships I would be remiss in not mentioning those whose love and friendship have formed me as I journey toward God: Sr. Maureen Michael Byrne, S.S.N.D., my "sister"; Sr. Louette Signorelli, A.S.C.J., whose effusive love has been an unmistakable sign of God's love in my life; Sr. Virginia Dunn, S.N.J.M., whose graciousness has contributed greatly to my understanding of God's grace; Neil Jarreau, S.J., who helped me to see that intimacy with God is all that really matters. I am grateful for Glenda and Sam Sinardi, Elaine and Brad Dewey, Grace and Richard Nelson, Anna Maria and Michael Gentile, and Kathy and Michael Nuechterlein who have supported me tirelessly; Angie and Henry Rojas, whose love uplifts me; Ruth Murphy, an ever-faithful friend, who daily reminds me of the total fidelity of God and whose help in the reading of this manuscript has smoothed out many rough spots; Sr. Lauriana Langevin, S.N.J.M., whose simple wisdom has inspired me. I wish to acknowledge with deepest gratitude the strength and support I receive from my sisters, the Sisters of the Holy Names of Jesus and Mary, New York Province. Emily and David Maney deserve special thanks for the computer that made the completion of this manuscript a much easier task than I had anticipated. I owe a great debt of gratitude to my colleagues at the Academy of the Holy Names and to those at the Academy to whom I attempt to minister, for their support, love and encouragement.

January 26, 1988
Feast of the Holy Name of Jesus

Table of Contents

Introduction

IN JESUS, GOD incarnated himself in our history and in human flesh: in our mothers and in our fathers, in our brothers and in our sisters, in our children and in our friends, in the rich and in the poor, in the weak and in the strong. The magnificent and overwhelming truth is that God not only dwells in cathedrals with vaulted ceilings, but also in flesh and blood people.

This little book is about people who are for others an experience of the living God. It is based on the premise that we can look at some of our deepest relationships and find there a clue to the unfathomable love of God. This is not a "how to" book for those who want to improve their relationships. It is about allowing the spiritual significance of our relationships to penetrate us, so that we will enjoy a truly religious experience in the sacredness of interpersonal union. It is about deep and genuine friendship with persons to whom we give ourselves with consciously sustained commitment. In using the term "friendship" throughout this book, I refer to conjugal friendship as well as celibate friendship, mindful that both involve deep levels of human intimacy.

This book is about the holiness to which each of us is called.

[xv]

God calls us to an intimate union with himself, and in so doing calls us to holiness. But holiness is never just ''God and me''; it is an interpersonal reality involving other people who offer us love on God's behalf and to whom we offer love on his behalf as well.

Growing up in Catholic schools, I ''learned about'' Jesus, his life and its meaning. It was not until what I had learned took on flesh and blood through the experience of friendship that Jesus became a personal reality for me.

Jesus' foremost desire was to bring us life: ''I came that they might have life and have it to the full'' (John 10:10). He sends us other people, friends, as sacraments of his presence, to bring us life. Perhaps in reading this book, you will be moved to reflect on those persons who have in their own way re-presented Jesus and have come into your life that you might have life! Perhaps you will recall those persons whose intimacy with the Lord has helped you to develop yours.

There are people in our lives with whom we may spend a great deal of time — co-workers, neighbors, members of our family, etc. — but too often we do not seem to realize that we actually share life with them; that there is a sharing of the richness of persons that issues from the richness of God. When there is interpersonal union, there is a transfusion of grace, a special sharing in the very life of God. There is always something in a genuine love relationship that is larger than that relationship. It is not something we own, it owns us. That ''something'' is a share in God's own life. What a wonderful God it is who not only allows us to share in his own life, but also uses the tremendous vehicle of human persons: arms that hold us, eyes that radiate with warmth, tender words, and shared laughter to bring us to experience that special grace-filled life.

God calls us to life, to holiness and to intimacy with himself. But we never come to God in a vacuum. We enter into intimacy with God by relating body, mind and soul to other human persons. God's love is operative in every experience of shared authentic human love.

Friendship
as
Sacrament

CHAPTER 1

God Is Here And Now

I AM CONVINCED that there are only two things in life that really matter: to know God and to be in love. Actually, these two things are one and the same. To know God is to be in love, and it is through being in love that we come to know God — because, as the Bible so beautifully puts it, "God is love." Our human relationships, if they are based on genuine love, are necessarily bound up with our relationship with a God who is love.

Christian life can be viewed essentially as an ongoing love affair with Jesus Christ who calls us to intimacy with himself. It is the one path to fulfillment. He is ultimately what we crave most, and it is only in God that our deepest yearnings are satisfied. One of the primary ways we see and touch God is through those whom he sends us. In them he is enfleshed. This God who is love has made love the basis for our existence. It is only in loving that we can experience the fullness of life, because true fulfillment issues only from God. Love gives life transcendent meaning precisely because love is God himself. Love cannot be readily defined within any other context apart from God. God is inexhaustible, unfathomable, all-encompassing — and so is love. Love is not something we "make"; it is a Person. Love is not "out there," apart from us. Love is in us to renew us constantly, to energize us and put us in touch with the very core of life by putting us in touch with one another.

The awesome ability of love to transform the very stuff of our lives can only originate in a source that is beyond the here and now. God's love transcends time and space. It is agape love, love that arises from God's graciousness; it is freely given and unconditional. In agape love, we love because the other person is; we love because of the be-ing of the other.

When we fully receive God into our lives, our love becomes agape. It is God's love flowing through us. Apart from God, we are capable of only eros. Eros is "love" that seeks to possess the other; its purpose is self-fulfillment. Agape, on the other hand, is selfless; it manifests itself in total dedication to the other's well-being regardless of personal cost. All agape love originates in the heart of Jesus. It would be well for the human lover to know God as a passionate God with a loving heart. As lovers, we should know the nature of the heart of Jesus because it energizes our own hearts. Basically, as a symbol, the heart points to the innermost part of a person, the love-center. It is the loci of passion, the resting place of grace. The Incarnation gives a heart to God. Throughout all eternity, God's basic intention was to enter into intimacy with his people; to call them to holiness; to communicate love; to communicate himself. His strategy was straightforward: he poured his love into the heart of his Son. This love was not meant to remain in Jesus' heart; it was meant to be passed on to all those who come to the Center. From the hearts of his disciples, Jesus' love would continue to flow. And so it continues even today. It is as if there is a transfusion of grace. That is, grace flows from one source, the heart of Jesus, through the channels of human hearts.

Our human loves can only be understood within the context of the love of a passionate God. God is not only a personal God who is deeply involved in each individual life, but he is also interpersonal. He not only exists in me and in you, but also between me and you, in our relatedness to one another. The love we share in human relationships is part of the grandness of a God who cradles us tenderly in his all-loving embrace. Whenever pure, selfless love is shared, we experience God.

All that we know about God points to his relational posture toward his people. We are called to maintain a deeply intimate posture toward him. This is the truly profound beauty of Jewish spirituality. For it is permeated with the desire to establish and maintain the intimate covenant relationship between God and his people. Because God is relational, life is an ongoing dialogue with him. God gives us time, space and other persons as a means of maintaining and deepening this dialogue. The Incarnation affirms this. It tells us that the way to God is through the human condition and that God suffuses all human flesh.

All aspects of the human condition are revelatory. Life is studded with moments of awesome recognition of the presence of God within certain experiences. Many times we speak of how some things are "coincidental." When we meet someone we have not seen in a long time in an unexpected place or circumstance, we call it a "coincidence." When we are thinking of someone and suddenly the phone rings and that person is on the other end, we call it a "coincidence." Well, I don't believe in coincidences. There are really no coincidences in life because God operates in and through our human experiences. He charges particular experiences with profound meaning and with the potential of impacting the very essence of life. These experiences are always vitally linked to relationships which are part of God's revelatory plan.

Each of us was conceived within the context of the relationship of our biological mother and father. We then entered into the intimacy of prenatal union with our mother in the womb, followed by the violence of birth and the first bittersweet taste of separation. But then came reunion through recognition. Our first cognition was actually a recognition. It was the recognition of a relationship, our relationship with our mother or whoever nurtured us. We recognized the warmth of arms that enfolded us, the taste of breasts that fed us and the familiar rhythm of breathing in the one who held us. In the rest of life, there are moments of union, separation, reunion and deep intimacy. Very often in these moments we experience something of the person of God. Fr. William McNamara, Carmelite monk and well-known author, puts it well when he says: "God does not act in a vacuum . . . He acts incarnationally through the marvelous, messy dimensions of our fleshy, dirty, wonderful world."[1]

Our faith is incarnational in that we believe that God is present to us here and now in the nitty-gritty of everyday life. The secret to securely living the Christian faith lies in understanding the Incarnation as an act of the God who is Emmanuel, God with us.

God is where we are. Our God is not simply present in the world in general; he is with us in a personal way where we are, here and now. His presence is not aloof and impersonal; it is deeply intimate: "Ever present in your midst, I will be your God and you will be my people" (Leviticus 26:12).

As human persons we must contend with all the demands of a confusing world and somehow not be overcome by them, but instead be consumed by God. The only way that we are able to live meaningfully within the complex web of the daily busy-ness of the world is by recognizing God especially in every face, in every pair of eyes and in every hand extended to us in charity. It is through other persons that we are mindful of the presence of God and touched by his divine love.

We are for one another the fulfillment of Jesus' promise: "I will be with you always." We embody that promise by being living sacraments of his presence for one another. We know that a sacrament is a symbol which offers us an experience of God's love in our space- and time-bound human life. While a sign points to something, a symbol makes present that which it points out. Therefore symbols can, if we allow them, affect us deeply because through them the presence of God emerges in our human lives and is intensely experienced. Sacraments are a part of God's plan because he deeply desires us for himself. It is God's desire to draw us to himself. Jesus articulates this clearly in the Gospel: "I — once I am lifted up from earth — will draw all people to myself" (John 12:32). It is God himself whom we experience in a sacrament. Our genuine friendships are sacraments because they are an embodiment and an expression of the reality of God's love. God loves us in an ongoing covenant of total fidelity. As a sacrament, friendship brings us in contact with this ongoing covenant here and now.

The point of sacramental encounter is that point at which the divine and the human meet. Put simply, God uses our human relationships to reach us; we experience him by loving and being loved by another. God reveals himself to us in the real life presence of those around us. The God of all history, the God of Abraham and Sarah, the God of Moses, the God of David, the triune God is enfleshed in those we call friends. The awesome ecstatic truth is that the all-loving God is truly present and active here and now in those to whom we relate in friendship. Gerald O'Mahony, in his unique catechism, *Abba! Father!* speaks of a sacrament as "a sign that makes visible the invisible God." He goes on to discuss how persons in union with one another can be mutual manifestations of God:

> You and I, disciples of Christ are sacraments, because our
> vocation is to make people who look at us say 'Ah, now I see
> what God is like.' We together can be a living and visible sign of
> the God that we can see (through Christ), but that the world
> cannot see.[2]

The basic mission of the Christian is sacramental. That is, we are called to BE the healing, tender, loving Christ in the world. We are not called to save souls. Christ did that once and for all. We are called to be signs of Christ's victorious resurrection and his ongoing presence in the world. We are called to BE Christ for one another. If we but open our hearts and minds in holy attentiveness to his Spirit, we will be "transformed from glory to glory into his very image by the Lord who is the Spirit" (2 Corinthians 3:18).

In that transforming process we will experience the sacramental presence of others within certain life experiences. Sacramental human experiences on the one hand have some value beyond the here and now, and on the other hand involve the presence and actions of those we call friends. These do not necessarily have to be elaborate or mysterious experiences. There is often deep inner truth to many of the simple things we encounter in a relationship: a big bear hug, an understanding glance, a special letter, sharing a can of beer, a walk on the beach together, or even a painful confrontation. Often they are vehicles through which we grow closer to one another, and in so doing come to know God better. Ladislaus Boros, in emphasizing that we reach God through one another, succinctly says: "Every lover experiences with a direct insight the reality of Christ."[3]   In all his magnificent wonder, God chooses to reveal himself through human persons.

God wants us to be in him, in Love, to be lovers. The term "lover" is too often used in its narrowest context to denote those involved in romantic love relationships. In the deepest sense, if a lover is one who lives an ordinary life charged with extraordinary grace, then all of God's people are called to be lovers.

Grace is key in the life of the lover. Grace is God's love freely given. It includes all the riches of God's gifts to us. Grace implies a relationship, the closest relationship possible. Grace is a relationship with God, an intimate communion of mutual giving and receiving. It is a relationship that begins at Baptism and grows and develops over time.

We have heard again and again that we are saved by grace, only grace. Nothing else can save us, not our good deeds, not our accomplishments, not even our piety. Only grace can save us. How magnificent is grace! God's gracious love has the awesome power to save us. The greatest gift we can give to another is to be a manifestation of that grace. The magnificent gift of grace is concretized in love that is shared. I have had the experience of being amazed that a particular person loves me, especially when I feel that I don't deserve the love. It is a free gift. It is given completely independently of what I have done. It is GRACE!

Often I am also amazed by the way that this grace flowing through another has the power to transform me. Real interior change only happens through grace. We can never really change by ourselves through sheer will power. It is the surging forth of God's grace that transforms our innermost being, making us holy.

God calls us to holiness. A person who is transformed by grace is said to be holy. A holy person responds to the world with deep faith, outrageous hope and abiding love. Holy persons are profoundly in touch with themselves, with the world and with God.

The call of the Christian is to intimate union with God. Holiness is the full entering into this intimate relationship with the God of love. Holiness always originates in God. As the second Eucharistic prayer at Mass so beautifully tells us, he is ''the fountain of all holiness.'' Holiness comes to us as gift from the outpouring of God's gracious love. Holiness is also a channel for God's grace to flow and transform the lives of others. As we journey through life we must open ourselves to receive God's gracious love, for when we receive it fully we enter into the realm of holiness. We cannot receive it alone; others facilitate our reception. Holiness, then, is an interpersonal reality. To be holy is to be in God, in Love.

In his book entitled *Holiness*, Donald Nicholl speaks of the significance of friends in facilitating our response to the call to holiness: "Everyone needs a soul-friend, someone who loves you so much that he will never allow you to stray from the path of holiness without both rebuking and encouraging you."[4]

Holiness is consummately social in many ways. It is the presence of a personal, loving God in interpersonal union with his people. Too often the idea of holiness conjures up a stale, dull and static image of plastic piety, when in reality it is a rich intoxicating experience of interpersonal love.

To see ourselves as holy is to recognize a potential for infinitely more than seems humanly possible. Holiness involves the presence of love at the center of one's being, at the "place" from which issues all that we are. Therefore, to be holy, we must be in relationship.

Interpersonal holiness is love originating in the heart of Jesus and flowing freely into and between human hearts. Interpersonal holiness is a human sacrament. It is the presence of the all-loving God in the here and now, in us and among us.

To be holy is to be charged with grace. Holy persons take part in a transfusion of grace. God's own love flows through us, and through us to others.

There is a certain tender joy about grace. To know God's gracious love is to be warmed by him and to enflesh God's own warmth so that we can bring it to others. God's grace is abundant; if we miss it, it is because of our own inattention. Through my interpersonal relationships, I have come to a new understanding of grace. I see more clearly how grace is woven into the fabric of my daily living. I have come to pray for the grace to BE grace for others.

Much of the charm of friendship is that we do not cause it to happen. It is a gift from God. Several years ago, I attended a ten-day education workshop in Boston. I arrived there with a heavy heart; I was burdened by some rather significant professional difficulties that had affected other aspects of my life. I went to Boston in need of healing, but with no expectation of being healed. I went to attend a workshop and for no other reason. Something very special happened to me in Boston that summer. It seemed as though what I had heard and read in Scripture and reflected on in prayer about the tender, soothing, healing love of God was overwhelmingly reflected in a person I came to know during my stay there. We became fast friends.

I came to believe as a result of that encounter that there is meaning in every meeting and that friendship is always a gift from God. In other words, we never "make" friends; we simply acknowledge what God intended for us since the beginning of time. I went to Boston with no idea of how my life would be touched by another person. I did not expect that I would see the very face of God there.

Abraham Heschel, that great Jewish theologian, tells how a child responded to the story in Scripture of the sacrifice of Isaac. Upon hearing that the voice of an angel stopped Abraham from killing Isaac, the child began to cry. The rabbi who was telling the story, puzzled by the child's tears asked: "Why are you crying? Isaac was saved." The child replied: "But, rabbi, what if the angel had come a second too late?" The rabbi comforted the child by saying, "An angel can never come late!"[5]

The story reminds us that when the time is right, God always sends someone who incarnates his love. God always saves us, and he uses others, "angels," as instruments of his tender, healing touch. Interestingly, the word "angel" is the ordinary Greek word for "messenger," someone who is sent.

Earlier I quoted Donald Nicholl's book, *Holiness*. The quote included the term "soul-friend" which Nicholl uses to describe those whom God sends us. He points out that a soul-friend is a "God-send" and that a soul-friend "has to be sent by God, because you can hardly advertise for one . . . God will send you a soul-friend, whether you like it or not; and then it is up to you to take the healing medicine she gives you."[6]   We do not schedule our relationships. It is God who works in time to bring us to encounter each other. We cannot predict when God will send someone; we can only wait. Usually, we cannot really even explain why two particular people are friends. It is a mystery grounded in God's plan for each individual person.

This mystery of God-sent soul-friendship can be clearly seen in the relationship of Jonathan and David in the Old Testament. Jonathan and David never intended to become friends. Actually, the possibility was quite unlikely since after all, Jonathan was the heir apparent to the throne and David was a poor shepherd boy from an unimportant family. Yet the two were drawn to each other: "By the time David finished speaking with Saul, Jonathan had become as fond of David as if his life depended on him; he loved him as he loved himself" (1 Samuel 18:1). There was some magic, some power beyond human understanding that brought these two to experience a special union. Jonathan and David's friendship involved a spiritual attraction that could not easily and logically be explained. They were soul-friends and their friendship was God's doing. It was a common love of God that specifically cemented their souls together.

If we believe that there are no coincidences in life, then we can begin to see that life is grounded in the idea of Providence. Providence implies that everything in the world serves a purpose that goes beyond the world: the purpose of the all-loving God.

To believe in Providence is to believe that there is special significance in everything that happens in the world, and that there is a loving God who looks out for the good of each individual person. In terms of our interpersonal relationships, to believe in Providence is to acknowledge that no relationship is accidental;

that all of them are guided by God's loving concern. It means believing that a long preparation, unknown to us, preceded those moments of deep encounter.

Sam Keen, in his rich and significant work, *The Passionate Life*, suggests that there is a "mystical harmony" that draws us together and binds us in meaningful relationship to one another. Keen explains:

> . . . the notion of chance, coincidence, or even synchronicity were threadbare philosophical garments constructed in a hurry to cover an embarrassing vulnerability in the armor of thinkers who are determined to be grown-up and reasonable at all costs. After all, "co-incidence" only means that two things happen at once — or come together. And coming together may be as easily a sign of a mystical harmony as a result of cosmic carelessness. If we remain at the level of experience, wild synchronicities seem the result of some special grace.[7]

It is the "special grace" of the God of love that makes love happen in our midst. The Spirit is given to us together, interpersonally. It is the ONE Spirit that brings us together in union: "The Spirit of the Lord fills the world, and holds all things together" (Wisdom 1:7). It is indeed Christ, himself, who binds us together.

The surging forth of love in a relationship should be an affirmation for us that the Spirit does indeed operate in our lives and especially in our relationships. St. Augustine writes: "True it (friendship) cannot be, unless in such as thou cementest together, cleaving unto thee, by that love which is shed abroad in our hearts by the Holy Ghost, which is given to us."[8]

Often we feel that it is by our own choice that we enter into intimacy with others — except, of course, our parents, siblings and other family members. The truth is that just as we did not choose

our parents, brothers or sisters, so too, our deeply personal friendships are not of our own choosing. All we did was to affirm God's
choice. Again, it is God's special grace that draws us to one
another. C.S. Lewis says it well:

> A secret Master of Ceremonies has been at work. Christ who said
> to his disciples 'Ye have not chosen me, but I have chosen you,'
> can truly say to every group of Christian friends 'you have not
> chosen one another but I have chosen you for one another.' The
> friendship is not a reward for our discrimination and good taste in
> finding one another out. It is the instrument by which God
> reveals to each the beauties of all the others. [9]

Awareness of the workings of God within our relationships
will eventually bring us to the realization that God continues to be a
part of any authentic love relationship. He is always between us
and those we love, not to separate us but to bind us ever closer
together.

CHAPTER 2

Friends, Prophets, Lovers

IF WE ATTEMPT to define human life or to search for its meaning, we will discover that our existence is really co-existence. Being in relationship with others is constitutive of truly being. We were part of an interpersonal relationship even before we were born. Basically, life is relational and friendship is a vital component of a full and holy life.

True friendship is mystery. It takes us in and captures us. We do not analyze it, but live within it and experience its fullness. It has a quality that speaks to the very core of a person about the sweetness and beauty of God. True friendship is inexorably linked to God. Aelred of Rievaulx put it beautifully:

> . . . friendship is a stage bordering upon that perfection which
> consists in the love and knowledge of God, so that man from
> being a friend of his fellowman becomes a friend of God accord-
> ing to the words of the Savior in the Gospel: 'I will not now call
> you servants, but my friends'.[1]

When our human friendships deepen, so does our relationship with God. The deepening of our friendship with God deepens our human friendships. In true friendship we help one another to stretch beyond our individual limitations and to reach for God himself.

Every relationship — whether it is with a spouse, a parent or a friend — has a spiritual dimension and can serve to deepen spiritual life. Friendship is often the realization of the Kingdom of God and of God's presence in our lives. Friendship is always a gift given to us to build the Kingdom. True friendship always draws us to reach out to others. It is a gift, not to be hoarded, but to be "used" and shared with God's people.

Each friendship we experience enriches every other friendship. Life is fueled by the energy that erupts from interpersonal contact. In friendship the whole person is uplifted toward God. As was discussed earlier, our friendships can be sacramental in that through a friend we can catch a glimpse of God. Also, we can be for one another an experience of God. God has given us the ability to mirror him; it is in friendship that this happens best.

Friendship is sometimes not given the position of importance in life that it should have, considering that it is essential to the realization of our full potential as persons made in the image of God. True friends complete us. They help us to define ourselves. They become a part of us and help us to be holy. Consider the words of St. Francis de Sales in his *Introduction to the Devout Life*: "For those who live in the world and desire to embrace true virtue it is necessary to unite together in holy, sacred friendship."[2]

Whenever I reflect on my own life and my relationships, I realize how much of who I am is linked to the people who have journeyed with me at some point in my life. We have all heard the speech given by the successful career person who strongly proclaims: "I am a self-made person! All that I have and all that I am, I have earned!" I would challenge that claim. I do not believe that there are any "self-made persons," in terms of the real successes of life like being a good parent or an understanding listener or a faithful spouse. As I examine my own real successes, I realize that I am certainly not a self-made person. All that I am and all that I have, I owe to those who formed me by loving, caring for and encouraging me. There have been certain persons in my life without whom I would be incomplete, less than the person I am. They are a very important part of my personal history and of my faith journey.

There are intense spiritual moments in our relationships which have enhanced our spiritual growth. While we may not remember the date or the time of these experiences, we can usually recapture their feel and taste long afterwards and rest in the realization that they have affected us at our center. It is through these loving persons in our lives that we cultivate a deeper, more refined love for life, the world and others. Our friendships are a school of love where we learn to relate in love to one another.

This truth was particularly impressed on me during my twelve years as a high school religion teacher. I can distinctly remember, during my very first year in the classroom, that there was a girl who never seemed to respond to anything when others attempted to be affectionate toward her. I was very puzzled about this, so I went to one of the school's counselors and asked about her. The counselor told me that this sophomore girl would not respond because she did not know how to. Though it has been many years, I can still remember the exact words: "Anna does not know how to love." The counselor went on to explain that Anna had been a foster child for most of her life, and that she had gone from foster home to foster home over the years. I was 21 years old then and very naive. I had come from an extremely loving and demonstrative family, and I took for granted that everyone knew how to love. I actually thought that everyone was born with this ability. It was through this experience with Anna that I realized that we learn to love by being loved. I also realized at the center of my being how very fortunate I had been to have come from an atmosphere permeated with love.

Unlike Anna, my growing-up years were a school of love in which through the lived experience of relating I learned to love myself and others.

We often hear people say that no one is indispensible. It truly bothers me when I hear this! Everyone in some way is indispensible! Each person has a totally unique contribution to make to others, a contribution that may be a key factor in the formation of a whole and holy person. We should stop speaking so much of believing in ideas, institutions and things — and start speaking about our belief in one another and in the friendships we share and the God who animates, sustains and dwells within them. To believe in another person is to acknowledge that they represent much more than meets the eye, that they are a channel of God's grace.

Friendship is a most human experience. Through our human friendships we are enriched and can enrich the lives of others. Our friendships are enriching precisely because the all-loving God dwells within them. Through them we come to realize more profoundly that God is present here and now, and that he continues to love us.

The significance of friendship became clearer to me once while I was participating in a group retreat. The retreat director asked us to map out our personal spiritual journeys by identifying milestone events on a time line. As I began to do this, I realized that in every instance there was a person (or persons) who played a significant role in that event and thus in my life. Every person has a personal spiritual story. Many people find it hard to pinpoint the personal realization of the dynamic presence of God in terms of an exact moment in time. However, that point is much more easily identified in terms of a person who speaks to us in God's name and beckons us forth to be fully ourselves.

Those persons who significantly impact our spiritual growth are for us prophets in a sense. If we consider the prophets of the Old Testament, we know them as persons to whom God had revealed himself in a special way so as to make them able to speak for God.

Prophets interpreted a people to itself, and ultimately sought to bring that people to focus attention on God.

There are still prophets today. There are not only prophets today who cry out for social reform and warn the people of the consequences of their lifestyles, but there are also personal prophets who enter our lives on an intimate basis and draw us ever closer to God.

We need personal prophets. We need individuals with whom we personally interact, whose obvious intimacy with God serves to instill in us a hope that, like them, we too can heed God's call and follow him to undreamed-of places. When we meet a person of radical hope who trusted God's promises even when they were unclear and led to pain and confusion, we are somehow given a new courage in following God's plan for us personally.

To be a prophet is to be a sacrament of God's Word. The "words" of some of my friends have been for me part of God's Word. As prophets to one another, we are called to speak words that do not go from lips to ears but from heart to heart. Basically, the prophets of old and our own personal prophets today announce the Good News — not so much in revealing the facts about Jesus' life and teaching, but in LOVING. Jesus saved us by grace, love freely given. It is the ongoing sharing of grace that renews the Good News in the human heart. Our personal prophets, then, have enfleshed the Word of God to such a degree that all they do and are bears witness to the reality of God's abundant love. They fulfill Jesus' words: "What fills the heart overflows through the mouth" (Matthew 12:34).

The Good News our prophets convey is that we are loved unconditionally; that redemption is a personal reality; that Christ redeemed each of us as a unique, individual person. We know that the resurrection has happened and that Christ lives today because we have met him in our prophets. They communicate this not so much with words and deeds but with the same presence that penetrated the lives of Zacchaeus, Matthew, the Samaritan woman and so many others. This presence touches us at a depth at which no one has ever reached us. We are touched by the realization that this person, this prophet is Jesus' promise kept: "I am with you always."

Our personal prophets see what we do not see, and are daring enough to share the vision no matter what the cost. There are times in our lives when we need new vision to see beyond the here and now. There are times when we dream tired dreams that never seem to come true. Personal prophets share their vision with us and call us to newness. It is much like what is spoken of in the book of the prophet Isaiah: "From now on I announce new things to you, hidden events of which you knew not" (Isaiah 48:6).

Each of us sees what no one else sees, in a way no one else can. It is shared vision that brings people to more vital contact with a broader spectrum of life and experience.

We wait for our prophets whether consciously or not, knowing in faith that God will send his messengers to bolster our spirits on our journey to him. We will recognize them because they seem as though they are "on to something." There is a sense of the holy about their presence, and a deep abiding love of God and his people.

God acts through our prophets to bring us to recognize a special strength within ourselves. In friendship we receive a special kind of life and power, but the relationship itself is not the source. The source is much bigger. A good, deeply personal relationship, grounded in God, is called into being by God. Because God is present in a friendship of persons open to him, the life and power in the relationship come from him.

Being an only child and having lost my father when I was 18, I often wondered what the inevitable reality of losing my mother, my last link to nuclear family relatedness, would be like. I often thought of that experience which seemed an inevitable though dreaded part of my future, and I shuddered inside. I felt I would never have the strength or the stamina to cope with the loss. That day of separation came two years ago. Now, as I reflect on it, I am still astounded by my own strength. I am certain that my strength did not originate in me. It came from a Source much beyond my own doing. It was Love that upheld me. From that day on I knew that Love with its power to uphold me, to strengthen me and give me courage is totally GIFT from the one boundless SOURCE: ". . . the love of God had been poured out into our hearts" (Romans 5:5). I came to the realization that when we experience the warmth and tenderness of love that flows from a relationship, and the strength derived from that love, it is overwhelming to think that God himself is acting.

True lovers go to the Source for all that they need to enter into a genuine, intimate love. True lovers spend time with the Source, become intimate with the Source and never separate from the Source. In a book entitled *Quality Friendship*, Gary Inrig expresses it well: "We learn to love, because we go to the source of love and spend time worshipping Him and learning from Him. If we do not worship well, we will never love well."[3]

We do not own our love. We never make a true offer of love to another that is totally our own. It is ours to the extent that we have received it from God. It is his love, divine love, and we are its channels.

While we do not own love, we should allow it to own us. Remember the movie "The Exorcist"? When the little girl became possessed by the devil, her whole being was transformed. Her facial features, her voice, her disposition all changed. She was possessed by evil, therefore she began to look and act evil. Imagine someone who is possessed by God, by love! To be possessed by God is to receive his love in our innermost selves, to bask in it, to allow it to penetrate our whole being, to act out of it, and to share it. It means allowing God into the deepest, innermost part of ourselves, filling our being with himself.

I've met people who are possessed by God. You have met them too. There is a gentle reverence about all that they do. You sense the holy even in the way that they butter their bread. Those who are possessed by God are in the truest sense lovers. Too often we reserve the word "lover" to refer only to those involved in romantic love. However, *all* of us are called to be lovers in *all* of our personal relationships. A lover is one whose life stance revolves around being selfless, caring and keenly sensitive to others. Lovers fully participate in life at the center and give 200% in their interpersonal relationships. Lovers are passionate persons in touch with God and with the people of God. Passionate lovers live with intense vigor, thrusting themselves wholeheartedly toward the God who IS love.

I am Italian! And I have always felt that Italians have an obligation to be passionate. I grew up with passionate Italians all around me. Actually, I am grateful to have learned to love early in life in an atmosphere charged with genuine and wholesome passion. To be passionate is to be on fire with love. Passion is what Jesus was about, and what he asks us to be about. It is what John the Baptist spoke of when he said that Jesus would baptize us "in the Holy Spirit and in fire" (Luke 3:16). Passion is what Jesus himself spoke of when he said: "I have come to light a fire on the earth. How I wish the blaze were ignited!" (Luke 12:49). Passion is what the traditional symbol of the Sacred Heart of Jesus is all about. The fire in the heart of Jesus is his burning, intense love. It is fire that evokes love in us. Once we meet this Lover-God we will be transformed. We cannot encounter fire and remain unscorched. We cannot experience God and remain the same. We will never be lukewarm again; we will burn with him.

The transforming intensity of knowing Jesus and allowing him to affect us is well demonstrated in the Emmaus experience. After walking on the road to Emmaus with Jesus and not recognizing him, his disciples realized it was Jesus as he broke bread with them. As their eyes were opened, the disciples commented among themselves, "Were not our hearts burning inside us" (Luke 24:32). Their encounter with Jesus was an experience of fire, and so they spoke of their hearts burning within them. We too can have an Emmaus experience whenever we recognize Christ in a friend, an acquaintance, a colleague, our spouse or anyone who offers love. We will know it is Christ because our hearts will burn with the fire of love, and that burning heart is a sure sign that Christ is present. It is at this point that we know by experience what it means to be passionate.

Jesus lived every moment of his life passionately. All that he did to affect the lives of others during his earthly mission gave evidence of the burning love in his heart. Examine some highlights from his life: he plunged into the Jordan at his baptism; he drove out the money changers from the Temple; he gave the blind man sight; he died on the cross. He did not do any of these things out of simple obligation or a sense of mission, but out of passion. He did them because of a passionate love for the Father and for the people the Father had entrusted to him.

Scripture also reveals to us something of the passion of the human spirit in the relationship of Jonathan and David. Throughout it, they showed forth their capacity to be persons of passion. There is particular evidence of this when the two parted company and wept. They wept, not just because of the pain of the separation, but out of passion. Their tears signaled their realization of the depth of their friendship, its grace, and its rootedness in the all-loving God. Perhaps what we need most today is this brand of godly passion, or at least the boldness to express the passion that is part of our legacy as God's people. It seems that in our fast-paced, often impersonal society, we have lost much of our passion. Jesus himself lamented the loss of passion in his own age: "We piped you a tune but you did not dance, we sang you a dirge but you did not wail" (Luke 7:32). Those who fail to embrace the passion that is theirs as the people of God are not deeply affected by joy or sorrow. God calls us to develop a deep passion for life, for being, as well as for the all-passionate God and his people. We are fully human, not when we think about love or study it or even emote about it, but when we become passionate lovers in tough, real relationships.

The key is to acknowledge the supreme Lover, to know him intimately and to love him with all of ourselves so that ultimately we can become like him. The Kingdom of God grows and flourishes whenever God's people enflesh his passion by acting with com-passion. The way of the Kingdom is the passionate way. When we pray "Thy Kingdom come" we are, in a sense, praying for ourselves that we might be receptive to God's love in our lives and thus be instruments of this love to others. The Kingdom issues forth where persons live in passionate union with God and with one another.

We are made for love; there is no fulfillment without it. The ministry of love is the one ministry common to all persons. With all the technologies, sophistication and complexities of the modern world, life still all boils down to one person loving another. When Jesus said "Love one another" he was asking us to fuss over and worry about each other; to respect, care for and become intimate with each other; to make excuses for, forgive, encourage, trust and cherish each other. He was telling us that fulfillment comes through the giving and receiving of unconditional love; that only love makes sense of life.

The popular Jesuit writer, John Powell comments that: "There is nothing else that can expand the human soul, actualize the human potential for growth, or bring a person into full possession of life more than a love which is unconditional."[4] Loving unconditionally is not a task of Christianity, nor is it an obligation. It is a condition of authenticity, of living life in its fullness.

Daily, I thank God for the fullness of my life and especially for gifting me with many wonderful things: talents, successes, the beauty of nature as well as the products of human ingenuity. He has gifted me with the ability to think and to feel and to enjoy, but God's greatest gift to me is undoubtedly his warm and tender love which I know through all the love-signs he sends me through human persons. His love is the one sure thing. Just about everything in life carries with it numerous conditions. Life is full of "if's." We know them well from all the products and services Madison Avenue offers. All of them sound wonderful, like an answer to our every need, but each one holds a "conditional, limited guarantee." Nothing is unconditionally guaranted for life except the love of God. Perhaps the most popular condition of our human loving is: "I will love you if you will love me in return." While we might never express that exact sentiment, it is often how we feel. God's love for us, however, is not dependent on our love for him. He loves us unconditionally, regardless of our response. God's love is absolutely ours, free, with no strings attached. St. Paul says it well: "For I am certain that neither death nor life, neither angels nor principalities, neither the present nor the future, nor powers, neither height nor depth nor any other creature will be able to separate us from the love of God that comes to us in Christ Jesus, our Lord" (Romans 8:38-39). There is certainly a great security in our full realization of this incredibly loving God.

Human love that is unconditional is God's own love enfleshed in and poured forth from the heart of a lover. In relationships where there is unconditional love we can experience the very security of knowing God's own love, because that human love is indeed God's love incarnated. For many of us the first glimpse of this security came from God's love embodied in our mother. In the intimacy of life in the womb, the unborn child experiences the total security of being connected to mother. After birth, there are moments of insecurity in the separation from mother, but there is a return of the sense of security for the child as he or she is pressed to mother's bosom. The love-signs — the feel of mother's warm embrace, the taste of breasts, the sound and feel of her beating heart, the rhythm of rocking — all bring the child the deep peace of security. Such a mother, whose body itself speaks love, is certainly an unmistakable sign of the presence of God. Later, when mother's arms are replaced by the arms of a lover, the understanding of a friend, the community called Church, the same God is present offering his unconditional love, the only source of true security.

This unconditional love is true agape love. If we love one another this way, our love will never die. Because it is love that is sanctified by God, it will pass into heaven glorified. We have assurance of this in the resurrection of Jesus, from which we are promised not only that we will have eternal life but also that his love has overcome ALL things. Jesus showed that love always wins. If we enflesh this love in our loves, we will always "win." Perhaps our winning is not what the world would consider a victory, but it is indeed a victory in terms of the things that really matter. St. Augustine's famous line, "Ama et fac quod vis," ("Love and do what you will.") touches upon this idea in that he is saying that true love is enough; all will work out in the end when genuine love prevails.

Jesus' brand of love that culminated in the resurrection and the victory of love is not sentimental. It involved hard core realities like dealing with life's ugliness: withered hands, blood-stained garments, leprous bodies. Jesus' love addressed nitty-gritty human needs: feeding hungry crowds, calming human fears amidst the thunder of a storm at sea. Jesus' love involved raw earthiness: he mixed dirt and spit to cure the blind man, he washed dirty feet and he died on a bloody cross. Lovers who want to be true sacraments of God's love can forget romanticism and instead live Jesus' brand of love: touching and holding the ugly as well as the beautiful; getting their hands dirty because in loving, dirt and blood and sweat and tears don't really matter.

The bottom line in fully living the Christian life, and thus being a living sign of the presence of God to one another, is always LOVE. Remember the famous questions from the Baltimore Catechism, "Who made you?" and "Why did God make you?" The answers: "God made me — to know, love and serve him . . ." really sum up all that we are called to do as Christians. The reason God made us was for intimacy with himself — and this comes through sacred intimacy with others. We will fulfill God's intention for our being if we live in close union with one another and give authentic witness to the reality of God's love in our world. On judgment day we will not be asked about our achievements, but about how well we have loved. We cannot take our academic degrees or our awards of distinction or our bank accounts into eternity. We can only take love. If we have not loved, we will enter into eternity empty-handed.

Life teaches us that NOW is the time to love: a minute, an hour or a day from now may be too late. There are many whose lives are dependent on our loving them into being. They need us to do for them what Jesus did for Lazarus: he loved Lazarus back to life. Lazarus was physically dead, but there are many in our midst who, though they are physically alive, are interiorly dead and in urgent need of someone to love them back to life.

I learned the lesson of the urgency of loving about thirteen years ago. I was a young teacher of Religion, and I was teaching a group of seniors in a Catholic high school. It was the third week of a new school year, a Friday, at the end of a school day. It was the end of a trying week. I was tired and so were my students. A few students were particularly disruptive and I came down on them. I announced to the class that I would assign an "F" grade for that day to those who had been disruptive. One of the boys affected stayed to see me after everyone else was dismissed. His name was Martin. Martin told me that while he was sitting with those students who had been noisy and inattentive, he himself had not been and felt that he did not deserve the "F." In a moment in which now I am certain I was inspired by the Holy Spirit, I told Martin that I believed him and that I would remove the "F." He was grateful and quietly left. I was the last person to see Martin that afternoon. That night Martin put a gun to his head and ended his life. Martin needed someone badly to love him back to life before it was too late. I still think about how I could have possibly saved his life. I thank God, even still today, for the grace of responding to Martin in the little way that I did. But daily I pray for the grace to see the depths of pain in the human heart, and for all that I need to be God's healing instrument for those in pain.

The bottom line is always love. It is the heartbeat of life. We love because it is absolutely right to love. We love because God is love. Popular author Morton Kelsey put it poignantly:

> Jesus explained that the reason we should be loving is not only for the good it creates and the joy it brings, but because by loving we share in the very nature of God himself. Love is the very warp upon which the fabric of the universe is woven. [5]

In genuine friendships woven in real love, we get caught up in the mystery of the communion of persons. Somehow our souls do not remain separate; there is a mingling of persons, two become as one. This communion is actually a sharing in the very life of the Trinity.

As God's people, we are persons in relationship to the Trinity. This relationship is constitutive of who we are. The life of the Trinity flows in us and through us to others. God calls us to see our lives within the context of this vital relationship, and at the same time to allow our relationship to the Trinity to define our relationship to one another. In an excellent book on the spirituality of married life entitled *Embodied in Love*, the authors put it succinctly when they say, "The intimacy between people that results from unselfish love is also the intimacy with Father, Son and Spirit that is the life of grace." [6]

How privileged we are to be able to participate in the very inner life of God through the magnificent vehicle of human relationships! In these relationships we can begin to know and love the three divine persons as they know and love one another. The love of the persons of the Trinity is so full that in reality we can speak of only one God. But this love is also solicitous and respectful of the identity of each member, and therefore we can speak of three distinct persons. Through the Trinity we are reminded of the individuality of persons as well as of their union in genuine human relationships. The mystery of this respectful intimacy draws us into the very presence of the Trinitarian God.

As was discussed earlier, meaning in life comes from intimacy with God. The peace we all seek comes only from this intimacy. This is what holiness is all about. To be holy is to give oneself totally to communion with God. The Trinity points to the interpersonal nature of holiness. Through the Trinity we know with certainty that God sanctified human relationships and that he is also a part of them. Where deep, genuine love is shared, God's grace is operative in a special way. In his monumental work, *Catholicism*, Richard McBrien confirms this idea:

> The mystery and doctrine of the Trinity means that the God who created us, who sustains us, who will judge us, and who will give us eternal life is not a God infinitely removed from us. Our God is a God of absolute closeness, a God who is communicated truly in the flesh, in history, within our human family, and a God who is present in the spiritual depths of our being and in the core of our unfolding human history as the source of enlightenment and of community.[7]

There is a special vitality in the Trinity that originates in the interconnectedness of the divine persons. Each person of the Trinity says ''yes'' wholeheartedly to the others' love. The Trinity is life-filled and life-giving. Because all love comes from God, the vitality of the Trinity flows in us and through us to one another. In recognizing this force within us, there is an urgency to share God's love and life outwardly. God calls us to embody in our human relationships the unity of the Father, Son and Spirit. It is this unity that Jesus prayed for in his Priestly Prayer: ''. . . that all may be one as you, Father, are in me, and I in you; I pray that they be one in us . . .'' (John 17:21). The unifying love shared in the Trinity was more than a significant influence in Jesus' life. It was at the very core of his being. Jesus was consumed by the Triune love and his ministry was basically about sharing this sacred love and bringing all of humankind into the same sacred relatedness.

Like the Trinity, we do not exist with one another independently but interdependently. We all share life from the same one Source; we all drink from the one life-giving "Fountain of all holiness."

When two people share in a deep interdependent relationship, they broaden and deepen their understanding of living and loving. Earlier, friendship was described as a school of love in which we learn to love by loving. Friendship is not an end in itself; it is a process, a part of our ongoing pilgrimage to God. Through our genuine friendships we deepen our relationships with still others. We are given the gift of friendship so that we can build the Kingdom of God. Friendship is a school of love in which we gain a keener perception of who we are and of how we operate within relationships — and so we learn how to better relate to others. We learn best through experience. Relationships are experience-filled and therefore create the scene for some very significant life-impacting realizations. In *Christian Life Patterns*, the Whiteheads address this topic briefly:

> One can look to one's own experience with a close friend to find examples of the overlapping of identities, the merging of selves, the intersection of lives that characterize intimacy experiences. Over time my relationship with a close friend provides a variety of situations which draw out and strengthen my ability to be with another person. My friendship thus both draws upon and further develops my capacities for intimacy. [8]

In the school of love we learn through experience (often painful experience) what is necessary to be a genuine lover in the style of God's own Son. Our friendships are certainly not a refuge from the rest of the world. They are instead a motivating force to reach out to more and more people in the world around us. As sacramental people, we are used by God to touch others. God expects us to share with others the love we have received from him. God himself is also a part of the process of our reaching out. Morton Kelsey says it well:

> This loving God makes only one demand upon us; he sends us out into the world to share with others the love we have received. Then we return to Love and slake our insatiable thirst for love once again. Then we go out again and help slake the thirst of others. [9]

The cycle of love is always giving and receiving. It always begins and ends with the Source of all love, Love himself. Once we thoroughly immerse ourselves in this cycle we will burn with his love and be impelled to bring others to experience the fire of God as well.

CHAPTER 3

Presence And Intimacy

T HE TRANSFUSION of grace flows through the channels of human hearts. It is through this transfusion of grace that we come to know God by experience. We know God through intimacy, through the presence, compassion, reverence and fidelity of others. We know him through the confrontations and affirmations of our relationships, through the sharing of personal stories, and through our physical selves.

Usually when we read or hear about ministry, it is connected with activity, serving by doing. But there is also the ever-important ministry of presence. To be present to another is to offer ourselves simply, freely, and totally just as we are.

Those who, in my own life, have brought me to see God more clearly and to better accept his abounding love, did it not so much with words or specific actions, but with a special presence. It was a presence that spoke of caring and loving louder than words could have ever spoken.

Two years ago, when my mother lay dying in a hospital room for four nightmarish days, I never left her side. A friend arranged to have a companion with me during the night and early morning hours. I had no idea who would be coming. The first night, while sitting on a chair very close to my mother's bed, I fell asleep for a brief time. At about 2 a.m. I awakened and saw a person seated in a chair on the opposite side of the bed. For a moment the figure was blurred. As I focused, wiping the sleep from my eyes. I saw clearly that it was an acquaintance by the name of Mary, someone whom I did not know well, but whom I had come to greatly admire from afar. I was awed that she chose to be with me to keep the night-watch during this intense time. Mary's presence was sacramental for me. It spoke beyond any comforting words anyone could have offered. Mary's presence was for me at once a sign and an affirma-tion of God's limitless love, a love that never ceases, even at 2 a.m. on the darkest of nights. I knew for certain and with every fiber of my being that God himself was present in that hospital room. On that night, through Mary, I caught a fresh glimpse of the all-loving God. On that night I knew God by experience.

Words, ideas and actions can be exhausted, but a presence cannot be. In the presence of another there is a wealth of energy flowing from God. So often words do not surface that are adequate and appropriate for a particular situation — but just to be present says much more than we could ever articulate with words. If you have ever stood at the bedside of a dying person, you know that often words seem absurd. But presence, even totally silent presence, says "I am here because I care." When we go to a funeral we sometimes attempt in feeble ways to console those who have experienced loss. I usually say very little at a funeral when I encounter someone who has lost a loved one, because I believe that my presence says more than I could ever say in words. It says that I cared enough to choose to be here; of all the places where I could be, I have chosen to be here and not someplace else. Presence is so important that often people travel great distances just to be present

— at a funeral, a wedding, a graduation, a birthday — because to bring oneself to another is life-giving and holy.

In our fast-paced, action-oriented society perhaps we need to develop a greater sense of shared presence. We need to learn to simply "be with" another person. Usually, we find ourselves calling friends and asking if they would like to DO something, to go to a movie or a concert or out to dinner. We ask our friends to join us in activities when all the time what we may have really wanted to say was "I want to BE WITH you." There are many people in our lives with whom we enjoy just being. There are those in whose presence we grow and feel especially good about ourselves. There are those whose presence is holy so that just a silent walk may be a healing and uplifting experience.

Perhaps, too, we need to develop a greater facility in being with God. For years it has bothered me that at Mass we say, "The Lord be with you," as if we have to plead with God to be with us. God, of course, is always with us; we are the ones who are not always present to him. Perhaps, then, we should say, "The Lord IS with you!" Perhaps, too, if we can become more comfortable in just being with one another, we can begin to realize that sometimes God calls us to just be with him, not to bombard him with words, mantras, thoughts and meditations. No, sometimes he just wants us to bask in his presence. Sometimes, at the end of a particularly trying day, the best I can do by way of prayer is to be with God. It is as if I say to him, "I have brought myself. It is the best I can do." At other times I just want to experience HIS presence while I make myself present to him.

Part of the great appeal of the movie "E.T." was that it spoke to us of our need to be with one another. E.T spoke to the little boy Elliot about "being with" him even though they would be physically separated. We were touched by the Extra-Terrestrial's words to Elliot at the end of the movie as the alien was about to depart: "I'll be right here." They seem to be an echo of Jesus' words as he was about to depart to the Father at the end of his earthly ministry: ''I am with you always.''

The desert experience of early Christianity was marked by shared presence. When people went to the desert fathers, they simply went to be with their spiritual directors. In their intimate exhange of shared presence, they found God.

Presence makes a difference. We will always need the presence of those who will stand with us through our sorrows and joys and all the ordinary moments of life. Those who stand with us and are totally present to us serve as powerful reminders of a God who never leaves us alone: "Ever present in your midst, I will be your God, and you will be my people" (Leviticus 26:12).

While the presence of certain significant others helps us to know God and grow closer to him, intimacy with others can serve to further strengthen our knowledge of and relationship with God. In this context, intimacy is an open and deeply personal sharing of self. Intimacy involves a radical trust in another and a willingness to reveal our very soul. In intimacy the medium of exchange does not have to be sexual intercourse. It can be, and more often is, a steadfast fidelity and an acknowledged, mutual vulnerability.

There is a scene in Morris West's novel *The Clowns of God* in which Jean Marie Barette (who has just become Pope Gregory XVII) visits a critically ill friend, Carl Mendelius in the hospital. Jean and Carl were very close; they were soulmates who had shared with each other the innermost secrets of their hearts. As Jean enters the hospital room where his friend lay dying, West presents a moving, touching and deeply spiritual scene:

> Jean Marie took Mendelius' hand. It was soft as satin and so weak it seemed that if one pressed too hard, the bone might crack.
>
> 'Carl, this is Jean. Can you hear me?'
>
> There was an answering pressure against his palm and more helpless gurgling as Mendelius tried in vain to articulate.

'Please don't try to talk. We don't need words, you and I. Just lie quiet and hold my hand . . . I will pray for both of us.'

He said no words. He made no ritual gestures. He simply sat by the bed, clasping Mendelius' hand between his own, so that it was as if they were one organism: the whole and the maimed, the blind and the seeing man. He closed his eyes, and opened his mind, a vessel ready for the impouring of the spirit, a channel by which it might infuse itself into the conjoined consciousness of Carl Mendelius. [1]

West goes on to say that the two men, simply united in silence, remained with their hands clasped for several hours.

This powerful scene is about intimacy. The two men had experienced the tenderness of intimacy. Even though Carl was only partially conscious, they experienced a renewed sense of their closeness, without words or gestures. Furthermore, Jean became a channel of grace for Carl. Through their clasped hands there was a transfusion of grace between the two men.

Intimacy involves a transfusion of grace, God's grace flowing from one person to another through the open channels of the heart. The experience of human intimacy, then, is an experience of God. The magnificent wonder of human intimacy is that the ties that keep us close to one another are rooted in the Holy Spirit of God himself.

William Johnston called intimacy ''a psychological necessity of life.''[2]   It is not only a psychological necessity, but a Gospel imperative as well. We can be neither real nor Christian without it. In intimacy we are so deeply touched by another that we become as one. We become part of each other when we enter into intimacy; something happens in our inner being that makes us MORE. There are many marks of human intimacy. We must never limit it simply to romance; it is much more. We carry with us a part of those with whom we have entered into intimacy. They become firmly woven into the fabric of our lives. In intimacy we name one another with silent words spoken in the depths of our hearts, and also with endearments we speak with our lips. For example, for me the word "Daddy" means more than a common name many children use to call their fathers. For me it signifies a deeply intimate relationship with a person whom I have loved with all of myself. To call my father "Daddy" was a symbol of our special connectedness.

We enter into intimacy with those with whom we dare to form an interdependent relationship. In interdependence, we recognize our limitations and our incompleteness as individuals and our need for others. We also recognize our need to be needed by others.

We enter into intimacy with those to whom we dare to reveal our deepest thoughts. Only a few people in our lives have such privileged access to our center. Few know the secrets of our innermost self, our yearnings, our true vocation, our struggles and our pain. In general, we are ready to speak of our worldly goals and aspirations to our acquaintances but we tell the secrets of our heart to our soulmates. With our soulmates we share the experience of knowing and being known. Heart speaks to heart and two are bonded together and become one.

We find fulfillment in intimacy, not because of some magic, but because whenever two people enter into human intimacy, God is operative in a very special way. The essence of God's revelation can be found in human intimacy because in such a relationship God is not an uninvolved third person, but is an essential part of it.

The ultimate relationship is one of intimacy with God. As salvation history unfolds, we witness the story of a God whose basic intention is to enter into intimacy with his people. This is basically what God is about. About six years ago I came to realize that all of life was about intimacy with God. In numerous sessions with a spiritual director, I attempted to discern exactly what was my primary life goal. It was important to me to arrive at something that was absolute. In this discernment, it became very clear to me that only one goal really made sense. I came to realize that there is in each of us an instinctive need for intimacy with God; that none of my deep yearnings could ever be satisfied apart from him. I came to fully embrace St. Augustine's words: "(Lord,) you have made us for yourself, and our hearts are restless until they rests in you."[3]

We are able to experience the sustaining joy of intimacy with God not by our choice, but because God initiated the relationship through Jesus: "Live on in me, as I do in you . . . apart from me you can do nothing . . . it was not you who chose me, it was I who chose you" (John 15:4, 5, 16). In all of John 15, Jesus' desire to enter into intimacy with us is evident. He no longer speaks of us as "slaves," but as "friends." The criterion for being friends is in-depth sharing: "I call you friends since I have made known to you all that I heard from my Father" (John 15:15). Jesus opens his heart not just to the disciples of his time, but to us as well — and he reveals not just thoughts, ideas and words, but himself. In our human relationships, mutual revelation and self-giving are the stuff of intimacy.

Often we speak of knowing something "by heart." In intimacy with God, we know him by heart. God is enfleshed in us, in our heart of hearts, and we dwell in the innermost recesses of God's heart.

This intimacy with God, so basic to our existence, flourishes in us as we develop human intimacies with one another. These prepare us to accept God's invitation for intimacy with him. When I experience moments of intimacy with a friend, I know it is the Spirit speaking to me in the depths of my being. I taste something of divine love in those moments. At the same time, the intimate relationship we establish with God will cause us to desire and work toward reaching out to others. In that way, perhaps we will also bring others into communion with God. The beauty of our intimacy with God shines through us and draws others to him. If our inner life is in harmony with God, our outward life will speak to others of the peace and joy that comes from intimacy with God.

I have known people who have established an intimate relationship with God and have dared to share with me some of the particular joys and sorrows of that relationship. Their union with God allured me and aroused in me a desire to want intimacy with him myself.

A willingness to be vulnerable must go with intimacy. It is quite risky to reveal to another the stuff of our souls. In so doing we allow another into our center, to see us naked, just as we are, no pretenses. We actually arm the other with weapons to hurt us. In this willingness to be vulnerable, there is an implied trust that the other will treat what we reveal with reverence and sensitivity. Through in-depth soul sharing, we reveal some things about ourselves — but more importantly, we share our very selves. To share one's true, deep, inner self can be more intimate than sharing one's body. It makes for a communion of human spirits cemented together by the Spirit of God. A friend and I have experienced the mutual sharing of inner struggles, and consequently we have grown closer. Often she has said that she believes that the Holy Spirit is "between us." I, too, have come to believe that in any genuine relationship there is a special place between the two where the Holy Spirit of God dwells and sustains. Again, the relationship of Jonathan and David in the Old Testament gives credence to this. Jonathan, in speaking of his relationship with David says, "The Lord shall be between you and me forever" (1 Samuel 20:23). The Spirit is between us, not to separate us, but to enrich the relationship, to sustain it and to make it holy.

The beauty of human intimacy is celebrated, reinforced and better understood within the context of the Eucharist. To receive Christ in the Eucharist is to experience the greatest intimacy possible. In the Eucharistic sharing we have the privilege of receiving God in such a way that he becomes part of us. The God of our salvation is so intimately united with us that we are one flesh with him. In the intimacy of the Eucharist we touch God and he empowers us to touch others. Thus we BECOME Eucharist.

When we pronounce "Amen" after the priest says "The Body of Christ" and holds out the Eucharist to us, we are not only affirming that this bread is indeed the body of Christ. We are also committing ourselves to BEING the body of Christ, blessed, broken and shared with others.

At the Eucharistic meal God calls us to friendship with himself and with one another. When we share the Eucharist, we unite ourselves as a community of persons to the divine; our human intimacy and our intimate relationship with God are blended. Somehow the Eucharist seems even more significant when I celebrate with close friends. With them, it seems I come to a deeper understanding of the meaning of Eucharist. This is because I share the bread that is Christ's body with the same persons with whom I share bread around the supper table, and with whom I share a word of love, the deepest yearnings of my heart, my innermost pain and my greatest joys. I know the meaning of Eucharist because I have suffered with and for another, and because I have experienced the consolation of those who have stood with me in times of pain and of celebration.

The words "Do this in memory of me" spoken at Mass do not just refer to celebrating the Eucharist in memory of Jesus within the confines of a particular time and space. They tell us that we must, in memory of Jesus, enter into the intimacy that the Eucharist so clearly symbolizes and makes real. At the Eucharistic celebration we are charged, in memory of Jesus, to love one another totally from the depths of our being.

True intimacy goes far beyond anything that we can discuss within the confines of words and language. It is a mystery we live, a mystery which draws us to the God with whom we share the ultimate, deepest intimacy.

CHAPTER 4

Compassion And Reverence

THE COMPASSION of others is but another way through which we come to more deeply know and experience the love of God. When we experience an enticement to go out of ourselves, to risk ourselves, and to become one with another human being, compassion happens.

Jesus was the enfleshment of the Father's compassion. The Incarnation was deeply personal in that it ushered God's compassion onto the human scene in a whole new way. God the Father's compassion became flesh in Jesus, and so now it must become flesh in us. Our basic mission as God's people is to articulate the nature and extent of God's compassion which is freely given to us. If we receive it with open arms it will enrich us to such a degree that we, too, can express the same compassion: ''He comforts us in all our afflictions and thus enables us to comfort those who are in trouble, with the same consolation we have received from him'' (2 Corinthians 1:4).

We can be compassionate only when we have come to terms with our own needs, weaknesses and dependence. We are broken people and our brokenness is basic to our identity. It says that we are incomplete, "not yet," in need of and dependent upon God.

Most often compassion gives us a sense of a common experience of broken existence. This feeling of shared brokenness is profound, but is not uncommon to the compassionate heart. In compassion we bear the pain of others; their failures, their hurts, their weariness, their fears become our own. This is why compassion is not a romantic idea; it is a tough, real act of loving. Jesus insists that compassion is much more than sentiment. For example, in the Parable of the Good Samaritan, Jesus defines compassion in specific, real, concrete terms: binding up wounds, pouring on oils, assuming the burden of another.

In compassion, while we forget ourselves and become one with another, we also come to recognize the unity of all people. In our compassionate response we say to another that, though we are unique as persons, at the center we are one with all people because we share a common, unifying Source.

Christ is at the center of any relationship formed in compassionate love. Where there is lived compassion in a relationship, we sense God's saving grace. The expression of compassionate love says to its recipient that life is about loving and that all of life moves toward the all-loving God.

Those whom we love become a part of us. That is why when someone whom we love is in a painful situation, we hurt too. It is as though through some mysterious intimacy, they are grafted onto us. Consequently, when someone we love dies, a part of us dies too. There is an emptiness, a holy void. That part of us will never be filled again, but that's okay. The void remains as a sign of our humanness and our willingness to allow someone into the innermost part of us. It is a sign of our compassion.

Jesus' charge to us is clear: "Be compassionate as your Father is compassionate" (Luke 6:36). The thrust of Jesus' life was to be compassionate as his Father was. The tough truth is that Jesus' compassion led him to the cross. Jesus' death on the cross was the ultimate expression of compassion. Jesus was so willing to identify with the brokenness of his people that he made himself broken. As his followers with extravagant compassion, we too must become broken. However, the power of brokenness that is formed out of a compassionate response to another's pain, can be overwhelming. It says that we are never alone; that God sends special messengers to journey with us, ministers of his compassion, to heal our wounds and mend our brokenness. It says that there is something holy about people, about life and about relationships.

The mutual, awesome recognition of a common personal experience often leads to an empathetic response. Passion becomes com-passion when the one who reaches out to us when we are in pain knows our pain and actually feels it with us.

The human heart is deeply affected by tenderness. Therefore God also uses the tenderness of another as a vehicle to reach us with his grace. When we experience this, we catch a special glimpse of the very heart of God, a heart that is full of tenderness and compassion.

To love tenderly is to be reverent. Reverence is a kind of holy respect combined with love and awe. We all deserve reverent treatment because in every person there is more than meets the eye. There is an infinite and inexpressible realm that is part of being one made in God's image. Basically, people are precious because they belong to God. Think of all the reverence we lavish on "things" belonging to God — holy objects, a Bible, a church — and rightly so. Sometimes we forget that people belong to God; they are holy by virtue of the fact that they were created by God in his own image and are animated by him. If we recognize one another's true identity as persons made in God's image, as holy ones of God, we cannot help but respond with reverence.

We are capable of reverent love because the love that resides in us is that love of the Trinity, three persons abiding in the depths of intimacy. It is the epitome of reverent love. We can love the way God loves: tenderly. Because God loves us, he draws us to himself, close to his heart. The first letter of Peter calls us to the same kind of reverence: ''By obedience to the truth you have purified yourselves for a genuine love of your brothers; therefore, love one another constantly from the heart'' (1 Peter 1:22).

For us to encounter God in another and for another to encounter God in us, a disposition of reverence is essential. Love cannot survive without reverence; it is the fertile soil where love grows and flourishes. I have been graced with persons in my life whose general reverence for life was so obvious, so real and so powerful that it affected me profoundly. With some people, their whole being speaks of reverence. There is a sense of reverence in all that they do. They seem even to be reverent when they ask you how you are or when they hold a baby in their arms. There is reverence in their kiss and in their words. These people have confirmed for me that there is something more to a person than flesh and bone; there is a heart and soul inexorably bound to the God of love. Their tenderness goes far beyond any human doings; it is grounded in a God who is the source of all tenderness and compassion.

The experience of the reverent love of another can create in us an inner compulsion to grow. This is especially true in marital love, but not limited to it. Reverent love allows the other the time and the space to be all that God intended. Reverent lovers invite us to see ourselves as valuable persons, loved by God. People tend to change in the continued presence of reverent persons. It happened to Peter, Mary Magdalene and Zacchaeus. Jesus' tenderness combined patience, firmness, acceptance and deep, abiding love to heal and transform them.

In reverence we are sensitive to the inner vulnerability of the other; we acknowledge that we are fragile, delicate and precious persons. In reverence we never possess another, because reverent love is freeing love. We never violate another's personhood by probing too deeply with questions. Sometimes reverent love falls silent in respect of another's need for quiet. Reverent lovers can always bear the silence in their relationship, finding a special comfort in wordless wonder.

The reverent lover recognizes the uniqueness of personhood, and through that recognition is awed at the magnificent beauty of God's people, made in his own image. When two reverent lovers meet, there is a recognition of a common life experience that issues from the one life-giving God. When they share intense moments together, there is a sense of reverence for all of life. In mutual reverence we cradle all of God's creations and creatures tenderly between us. Persons of reverence open up to us a world charged with gentle beauty. Through their eyes we can see a new calmness in a beach bathed in moonlight, or experience a renewed sense of awe before the reality of a God who nourishes us with his body and blood.

Reverent lovers make us feel loved in a special way. Their love is nurturing love. An offer of love that is tender and respectful of who we are says that we are special and lovable. In the face of that loving statement, and relying on its constancy, we can grow and become more fully the persons God intends us to be.

CHAPTER 5

Fidelity

IN AN ERA of broken promises, for-
gotten commitments and failed relationships, we can come to know
God also through the fidelity of others. In our world, only God
stands out for us as the Someone who will always be there, no
matter what. He is a God who remains faithful through all our
infidelities. The hallmark of Jesus' life is the resounding "yes" he
speaks with his whole self. His "yes" to being the Son and to doing
the Father's will means everything to us. Jesus' "yes" was life-
giving and redemptive; it gave us the gift of eternity. Our God is a
God of yeses that are never revoked by our noes to him. God has
bound himself to us for all eternity with a covenant of lasting
fidelity. Even before we were born, he began a love affair with us
rooted in this total fidelity. A friend who remains faithful through
all our ups and downs keeps the ideal of God's total fidelity visible
and real in our lives.

Through our human relationships, our covenant relationship
with God deepens and develops. This is not a static encounter with

God. It is constantly renewed and deepened throughout our lives. Through our fidelity to one another we cooperate in Christ's work of redemption and so bring God to birth within ourselves and within our relationship.

The undercurrent of all spiritual life is fidelity: to self, to God and to others. To be unfaithful is catastrophic. A broken vow is tragic. A life lived without commitment is a life wasted.

We readily think of commitment in marriage, but we do not often speak of commitment in friendships. Yet in every deep friendship there is a commitment, often unspoken, but nonetheless real. Any deep and genuine friendship is rooted in a covenant between the two persons. There is a point of surrender in every relationship. Once that point is crossed, the persons involved are committed forever. Of course, some relationships never reach that point. Friendship covenants, unlike those of marriage, are not formally initiated. Ironically, as children we recognized the value of formally sealed friendships. I can remember as a child going through the ritual of becoming a "blood sister." I hated the idea of pricking my finger with a pin so as to allow blood to flow, but I did it because it meant I would be specially bonded to my friend. As adults, we have pretty much eliminated such rituals. Nonetheless, the intent to be bonded in everlasting commitment to another is there.

The idea of "covenant" is one of the most important concepts of both the Old and New Testament. A covenant was, of course, a most solemn and sacred agreement which bonded two parties to each other. Through the Sinai Covenant, the most significant of the Old Testament covenants, the Israelites became Yahweh's own out of all the people of the earth: "I will be your God and you shall be my people." The Sinai Covenant is sealed in the ritual of the sprinkling of blood signifying that the contracting parties have become one blood, one family. The covenant is the ultimate seal of Yahweh's faithfulness to Israel. The New Covenant is sealed in the blood of Jesus. As an extension and a renewal of the Sinai

Covenant, for us it means that God will always be faithful. It is not written on stone tablets as was the Old Covenant, but on our hearts. It is a deeply personal covenant.

It is our covenant relationship with God, this most sacred of relationships, that sustains us through all of life's ups and downs. I am astounded at the faith of the Jewish people who were about to be put to death in Nazi concentration camps. I remember reading that those people, knowing that they were about to die, sang praise to God as they approached the gas chambers. They were able to praise God even in the face of death because they knew that he would ultimately never abandon them. Even though they were to die, God would still be faithful. It was their radical belief in their covenant relationship with God which sustained them. We are sustained by a covenant relationship with that same God. In entering sacred, covenantal bonds with one another, we come to understand our covenant relationship with God more fully and we are able to be more faithful in upholding our part of the agreement. Basically, our human friendships which are rooted in a deep covenant agreement, whether explicit or unspoken, give us a greater sense of the God who is always faithful. We can more deeply experience a sense of our covenant destiny with God by entering into sacred bonds with one another.

Covenant relationships always operate on faith. We "believe in" those to whom we commit ourselves. To believe in someone is to give that person your heart, the very core of your being. We give each other a heightened sense of self-esteem, not through some dramatic, sensational act of love, but through the steadfast act of relentless belief in another day after day, acknowledging all the other's potentials and possibilities.

Faithful people believe in us in such a way that their belief enlivens us. Jesus believed in Lazarus so much that his love brought Lazarus out of the tomb. The Father believed in Jesus to the degree that he brought him back from death to new life. When we experience physical death, God's belief in us will also bring us back to life.

Once again we can look to the relationship of Jonathan and David for a deeper understanding of interpersonal fidelity. Jonathan and David radically believed in each other. Each saw the other as one committed to God. True, in-depth human commitments can only be made by those whose lives are firmly grounded in faith and in a covenant relationship with God. There is evidence of this in Psalm 27. When David says, "Though my father and mother forsake me, yet will the Lord receive me" (Psalm 27:10), he is referring to his reliance on God. In the wilderness, David had forged a deep and lasting relationship with his Shepherd; he had learned to rely on God in all of life. Jonathan's life and his spirit of self-giving testify to his radical belief in the One who was his ultimate Sustainer. The two then, at the deepest level of their loves, held a common radical belief in God. Each could give the other his heart because each recognized that the same God of their longings dwelled there. For us, to believe in another is to first see that there is something more to this person than a simple human presence. To believe in another is to recognize that God himself breathes within us all and gifts us with unimaginable potential to be fully the persons he intends us to be.

Part of Jonathan and David's commitment to each other involved radical trust. Jonathan risked everything for David because he trusted David's love. Jonathan was caught between his father, Saul and David. Saul wanted David put to death, and Jonathan was aware of his father's intentions. Jonathan told David of his father's plans, and he went to his father and spoke highly of David. His loyalty was so outstanding that he became intensely involved in David's problems. Jonathan's involvement, however, became very costly. At one point Saul actually tried to murder Jonathan for his support of David. In his bearing of David's burdens, despite the cost, the breadth of Jonathan's commitment is evident.

Jonathan willingly risked everything because he loved David and because their covenant relationship meant that they trusted each other radically. Jonathan knew that even though he might lose his life in the process, he would never lose David's love. David, on the other hand, trusted Jonathan to always be there, to stand by him in all his trials. The important thing, even beyond their radical trust in one another, was that they entrusted each other to God as well. Jonathan was a channel of God's strength for David. In entrusting David to God, Jonathan taught David to depend on God. David depended on Jonathan's loyalty and saw in it something of the total fidelity of God. God was so much a part of their relationship that when they were faithful to each other, it was at once an expression of their faith in God. Jonathan speaks of "the Lord's bond" between him and David. It was this bond that not only united Jonathan and David to one another, but also bound them to God. Their dependence, then, was at once a dependence on each other and on God. The knowledge of their mutual fidelity and their faith in God is what sustained the two men when they parted company. After leaving Jonathan, David had been externally betrayed by the Ziphites, but internally he clung to God: "Behold God is my helper; the Lord sustains my life" (Psalm 54:6). God's strength sustained David. Jonathan was a channel of that strength for him.

Another Old Testament story beautifully illustrates how our human fidelity can be a reflection of the great fidelity of God. The story of Naomi and her daughter-in-law, Ruth, offers us a profound example of what it means to be faithful in a relationship. As the story unfolds, Naomi, her husband Elimelech and their two sons move to Moab where Elimelech dies. Their sons marry Moabite women, Ruth and Orpah. Later the two sons die, leaving their mother, Naomi, in a foreign land with her two daughters-in-law. Naomi decides to return home and counsels Ruth and Orpah to return to their mothers and marry again. Orpah returns home, but Ruth, because of her deep devotion and fidelity will not leave Naomi.

At the parting of Orpah, we read, "Orpah kissed her mother-in-law good-bye, but Ruth stayed with her" (Ruth 1:14). At the critical moment, Orpah decides to go it on her own and leave Naomi, but Ruth "stayed with her." Some Bible translations use the word "cling": "Ruth clung unto her," as a man "clings to his wife" in marriage (Genesis 2:24) or as the soul "clings fast" to God (Psalm 63:9). Earlier, the passage mentions that Ruth had also kissed her mother-in-law. Both daughters-in-law kissed Naomi, but how different their kisses were! Some kisses carry with them a profound message of fidelity and love, or even an offer of life. Some are shallow or even empty. Orpah's kiss expressed an emotion, but Ruth's expressed the fidelity of her heart. In friendships, some people only journey part of the way with us, as did Orpah. They reserve the right to leave. There is always a backdoor in some relationships. Ruth was willing to stay. In staying, she entrusts her life to Naomi and through Naomi to God. In this act of fidelity, Ruth gained everything, for through it she became the great-grandmother of David, an ancestor of the Savior of the world.

It is fascinating to note that Naomi, out of concern for Ruth's future, did not want her to stay. In answer to Naomi, Ruth speaks the magnificent, now classic lines, "Do not ask me to abandon or forsake you! for wherever you go I will go, wherever you lodge I will lodge, your people shall be my people, and your God my God. Wherever you die I will die, and there be buried" (Ruth 1:16-17). These are certainly words of total fidelity!

What is most interesting about Ruth is that prior to her association with Naomi, she did not know God. She had grown up as a pagan Moabitess. It was the love of Naomi and her family that drew Ruth to Israel's God. Ruth had tasted life in a home that worshipped Yahweh. This experience probably figured prominently in Ruth's decision to stay with Naomi. After having tasted something of the wonder of God, Ruth could not go back to the ways of pagan Moab.

Naomi was for Ruth a sacrament of God's presence, a channel of his love. Naomi must have realized this, and also must have experienced something of the wonders and goodness of God in Ruth's total and powerful fidelity.

Our human fidelity, then, can be a reflection, although sometimes faint, of the total reliability of God. We work in partnership with God at cultivating deep commitment. In so doing, we transcend the here and now of our relationship and move into the realm of the mystical. When we experience a true sense of deep and genuine fidelity in a relationship, we experience something of God. William McNamara said it well: "Falling in love may be romance, but staying in love is mysticism."[1] In a relationship based on mutual fidelity, there is always a promise. It is a promise that there will always be something more in life; that there is Someone who is more than we can imagine.

CHAPTER 6

Affirmation And Confrontation

B EING AFFIRMED and even confronted by another can also be ways in which we come to know God by experience. All of us have a need to know that we make a difference to someone. When we learn this through the words and actions of another, we are affirmed. The human affirmation we receive from another is a sure sign of God's action in our lives. Our greatest affirmation comes from knowing that we are known, accepted and loved by God. But God's loving affirmation has to enter our lives in a concrete way that we can understand and with which we can identify. Human affirmation is a vehicle through which we come to know and experience the affirming love of God. God loves us unconditionally, totally, without any reservations, just as we are at the present moment. That is a hard reality to believe. We come to believe it when we experience the acceptance of another human being.

A friend is a bearer of the good news that we matter! Through affirmation we have a great power over another. When we choose to give or not to give affirmation to another, we exert a great deal of control over that person. Earlier the concept of loving someone back to life was discussed, using the example of Jesus with Lazarus. The affirmation we give is a way of loving another back to life. Affirmation is life-giving and we hold its power within our hearts.

Affirmation urges us to be all that we can be. John Powell addresses this idea succinctly in his book entitled *Unconditional Love*: "I become a person only if I receive my personhood from someone else through the gift of affirmation."[1]   It is as though through loving affirmation we give birth to another anew and share with God in the process of creation. As sacraments of God's loving affirmation, we approach others and help to bring them to full potential. Bernard J. Bush, S.J., in his sensitive book *Living in His Love* goes so far as to say that "the work of creation is always unfinished, and it cannot be finished until we affirm one another into that completeness of the work God has begun. In a special sense, we stand in the role of God toward one another."[2]

In friendship we complete God's work by affirming the be-ing of another. As co-creators with God we say to one another: "It is good that you exist!" We actually protect others from themselves, their guilt, poor self-esteem, fears and anxiety. When people feel dejected and worthless, they cannot regain a positive sense of themselves through reading books, nor even from pious spiritual practices. It is only through the affirming touch of another human being that persons are brought to know and love themselves more fully. In genuine friendship each sees the tremendous possibilities in the other. Each urges the other to discover their true self and thus grow to the full potential that God intended. Self-knowledge coupled with a deep recognition of self-worth, does not come from self-scrutiny; it is a gift from God channeled to us through those whom we call friends.

We can affirm another by simply "being there" always, as a reminder of God's ever-present love and affirmation. The knowledge that our friends are there and believe in us, endorses our dreams for ourselves and motivates us powerfully to become all that we can be.

There is a magnificent passage in *Meeting God in Man* by Ladislaus Boros, S.J. in which the affirmation power of friendship is discussed:

> In friendship there is an unconditional affirmation of being. Its essence consists in saying: You shall unfold all the potentialities of your being; you shall even become still more beautiful, more radiant, more powerful and more alive than you are; you are the world for me; I experience the world truly only in the light of our friendship; a world without you would be a world without beauty for me.[3]

Friendship that manifests something of the love of God is not always just an experience of affirmation. Often we are disturbing elements for one another. Sometimes genuine friendships call for confrontation. Confrontation can be very disturbing, especially as it tends to unmask illusions and reveal deep truths. However, confrontation with pure intentions tempered with compassion can be a way of helping the other person to grow and blossom. It can be a tremendous revelation of God's love and concern for the individual.

In an experience of confrontation, the person doing the confronting may appear to assume a position of moral superiority over the other. In confronting another, we communicate to them either directly or indirectly that we have a better perspective on the situation at hand. Considering this, a loving, genuine friend would be reluctant to confront. However, reality tells us that one person does know better than another in certain instances. There is then a moral imperative to confront. Of course, the decision to confront first requires a keen understanding of the human spirit and prayerful discernment. The moral imperative is to help another to grow and develop. M. Scott Peck, M.D., noted psychiatrist/author stressed the obligation of friends to confront one another in his popular book, *The Road Less Travelled*:

> To fail to confront when confrontation is required for the nurture
> of spiritual growth represents a failure to love equally as much
> as does thoughtless criticism or condemnation and other forms of
> active deprivation of caring.[4]

Whenever I think of loving confrontation, the story of Nathan and David in the Old Testament comes to mind. Nathan was a clever but loving prophet who confronted David for committing adultery with Bathsheba and sending her husband to his death. Nathan tells David the story of a rich man who had numerous sheep, and of a poor man who had only one lamb which was his pet. As Nathan's story goes, the rich man had a visitor for whom he wanted to provide a meal. Instead of taking a lamb from among his many, he took the poor man's pet to feed his guest. Upon hearing the story, David reacted with great anger to the rich man's behavior and announced that the rich man deserved to die. Then came Nathan's sobering words to David: "You are the man!" Nathan goes on to remind David of how he took Uriah's wife and killed Uriah with the sword of the Ammonites. David then realizes that HE is the rich man of the story. In this confrontation Nathan moves David to see and to repent. It is out of love that Nathan confronts David, and it is that love which brings David to realize the gravity of his sin and ultimately causes him to grow. Nathan was sent by God; he is truly a prophet, one who speaks for God. Through Nathan's loving act of confrontation, he is for David a sign of God's concern.

I have known a few Nathans in my own life experience. There have been those personal prophets whose gentle confrontations have moved me to change and to grow. Their wisdom has led them to believe that confrontation is sometimes the most loving thing to do. They follow the example of Jesus who spoke many tough words of confrontation to the Pharisees, the Scribes, the woman at the well, and many others. His words penetrated to the core and affected his listeners deeply.

Both Nathan and Jesus were sent by God to touch his people. We too are sent by God as his representatives — to re-present him to his people. Our representation is characterized mainly by love — and sometimes confrontation is the best manifestation of that love. A true friend is willing to lovingly approach a friend with the truth even if it may hurt that person. While it may be difficult, confrontation can be a necessary part of the friend's growth. Basically, confrontation can be an expression of compassion — provided, of course, that it is not motivated by any sort of selfishness.

Through confrontation and affirmation, friends lead us in directions we may have never dreamed we would go. Perhaps we need to gently confront one another more often and thus move each other to greater growth. And perhaps we need to experience more embarrassing moments in which we celebrate one another in admiration. Certainly, we need to speak words of affirmation for each other long before the funeral eulogy. In these experiences of affirmation and confrontation, we can once again catch a glimpse of the all-loving God.

CHAPTER 7

Sharing Our Stories

ANOTHER UNIQUE WAY by which God is revealed to us is through the sharing of personal stories. The unique yet common nature of every human story was impressed upon me one warm summer day about four years ago. I was standing at the subway exit to the World Trade Center in New York City during rush hour. Suddenly a sea of faces came streaming out of the depot area. I began to reflect on what I was seeing. There were tall people, short people, fat ones and thin ones. There were men and women, some in business attire, others in jeans and T-shirts. However, my reflections had little to do with what these people looked like. I was thinking about how all these people, with varied appearances and statures, representing numerous ethnic, religious and socio-economic groups, carried with them as individuals a whole universe of unique experiences. It suddenly seemed awesome to think that each of these hundreds of people had a personal and unique story.

All of us carry within ourselves a personal story. All those persons who have impacted our lives, those who have loved us and those who have refused to love us are within us; somehow they are a part of us. In each of us there lives a mother and a father, a betrayer, a childhood friend, a teacher. They are part of our story, and it is our story that gives shape to our lives. Personal stories are but another way that God chooses to bring us ever closer to him. Our personal growth depends to some extent on how much in touch we are with our own stories. It is also important that we know our father's story, our mother's story, our spouse's story and the story of anyone with whom we come into vital contact. Their stories can lend meaning to our story, and can even be instrumental in shaping our lives.

The deepest realities of human life cannot be defined in intellectual terms. We can, at best, touch on them through stories. So many of the intricacies of human love and the responses of the human heart to it can never be adequately grasped in words of explanation or description. Very often they can best be understood within the context of a story.

Stories are meant to be shared; shared personal stories uplift, teach and even transform the listener. Our stories are only made meaningful in the ear of another who accepts and understands us. When our friends share their personal stories with us, their stories give flesh to abstract ideas. Their stories help us to understand the world, other people and life itself. Basically, they put us in closer touch with the reality of the human condition because they speak to us of the true drama of life, its joys and struggles.

The stories that are most descriptive of who we are, truly are stories of relationships. It is those experiences within relationships that shape our human stories. We bring our relationship stories to all that we do. When I hold a crying child, I bring my childhood experiences of brokenness and hurt. I say with my whole being that I, too, have suffered. When I am able to listen attentively to a hurting friend and to offer words of comfort, it is because within my own personal story I have been listened to and comforted. When I am able to wholeheartedly celebrate with others over their joy, it is because my own personal story includes moments of intense joy.

Basically, our human stories are stories of God. Because we are made in God's image, because he is always operative in our lives, and because we belong to him, we cannot separate our personal stories from God's story. Our stories are actually a recounting of our personal and collective journeys toward consummate union with God himself. God's story is the story of a magnificent love affair. It is the story of a God who falls so deeply in love with his people that he gives them the gift of his Son. Because our stories and his are intertwined, our stories are always love stories too.

CHAPTER 8

Touching God

MANY TIMES this little book has
discussed how we can come to know God through those people in
our lives who offer us love; how God himself speaks to us in the
persons of those who touch our lives. Often it is the personal stories
of such people that bring us into closer contact with God and help to
shape the stuff of our own stories. Our friend's stories and our own
stories are essentially God's stories of how he works through
human persons to touch and to transform human lives.

Thus far this book has discussed how we can experience God
through the presence of another person, through intimacy compassion, reverence, fidelity, affirmation, confrontation and
personal stories. We also experience God in a very specific way
through our physical selves. In the sensuous experiences of life —
in touching, seeing, hearing, tasting and smelling — we can
experience God.

We often think of spirit, mind and body as interconnected in
the human person. Actually, there is more than just intercon-

nection; the spirit is diffused throughout every cell of our mind and body. God breathed a living spirit into the newly-created human form, bringing to life a totally integrated person.

Unfortunately, in our society the concept of sensuality is too often solely associated with the idea of sexual activity. In its truest meaning, sensuality implies the full use of all the gifts of the physical self that God has given us. We can use these gifts in a very beautiful way to bring others closer to God. All that is sensual is simply pleasing to the senses, and such things remind us of their Creator. God made us for pure, holy sensuality. That is why we experience a wholesome pleasure when we swim or smell lilacs or eat corn off the cob. The moving sounds of a Mozart sonata, the smell of fresh baked bread, the feel of a cuddly puppy or the sight of someone we have not seen in years can be experiences of God. Through all these sensual things we celebrate our Creator.

Certainly God is experienced in a warm embrace and not in a neon sign; in a sunset and not in a Cadillac. The God we experience is not cold and aloof, but sensitive and sensual. Jesus is so obviously sensual that he was accused of being a glutton and a drunkard. He was moved by the heartbroken widow of Naim and by the death of his friend, Lazarus. He often spoke of sensual things like sheep, birds, lilies, mustard seeds, fire, lepers and little children. He chose to become bread and wine so that we could see, feel, smell, touch and taste him.

Being sensual is essential to being holy. Recognizing and embracing the sensual puts us in touch with one another and — as has been mentioned time and again — through one another we come to know God better. Matthew Fox, in his book *Whee! We, wee All the Way Home*, speaks of a "sensual spirituality" as one that praises God for "creating and continuing to create the sensual experiences of: touch . . . sight . . . hearing . . . smell . . . taste."[1] In a way, all spirituality is sensual in that our spiritual experiences involve all that we are, body and soul.

We experience God in sensuality most poignantly through experiences with other sensual human beings. We need not speak of any deep sexual experiences to understand how God reveals himself through human sensuality. God reveals himself to us in the warmth of a glance or the radiance of a smile, in a welcoming hug, in shared tears. I have a friend with magnificent, true blue Irish eyes that speak warmth, caring, understanding and affirmation, without words, just eyes in which God himself is reflected.

In a special way, God reveals himself to us in another's touch. Touch represents a potent force from life in the womb until death. Human touch actually has a nurturing power. Research has shown that touch is the earliest of the human senses to develop. A significant amount of tactile stimulation occurs in the womb: there is the constant stimulation of the skin from the amniotic fluid and the pressure from the walls of the womb. In the early stages of physical and mental development, touch is vital. Studies indicate that infants who experience extensive, loving physical contact learn to walk and talk earlier than those who have little such contact. It has been demonstrated that deprivation of loving physical contact has even resulted in death for an infant.

There is little doubt that touch is essential to an individual's healthy physical and mental development. Affirmation, trust and love flow from warm physical contact with another person. This is obvious in the little boy who clings to his mother's hand and even tries to bury his face in it; in the patient in a hospital bed reaching for the hand of a friend; in a firm handshake to seal an important agreement; in a warm embrace that soothes a crying child. This sense of security is experienced in the intimate body contact of sexual love and in the big, welcoming bear hugs used to greet a long-absent friend.

God is a God of touch. The Gospel portraits of Jesus present him as being not only tender, loving and deeply compassionate, but also sensual. He resorts to the sense of touch to bring others to better grasp the Father's love. Jesus cured the sick and lame by laying hands on them. In curing a leper, Jesus "stretched out his hand to touch him" (Luke 5:13). When the little children were brought to him, it was "to have him touch them" and Jesus "embraced them and blessed them, placing his hands on them" (Mark 10:13,16). When Jesus cured Peter's mother-in-law, he first "took her by the hand and the fever left her" (Matthew 8:15). When Jesus raised Jairus' daughter from the dead, "He took her by the hand . . ." (Luke 8:54). There is also the account of the special touch of Jesus as he washed his disciples' feet (John 13:1-17).

There are also several instances in the Gospels where Jesus is the recipient of another's touch. There is the anointing of his feet by the penitent woman. There are the accounts of the crowds coming to hear Jesus and to be healed pressing around him and trying to touch him. And, of course, there is the classic example of the woman with a hemorrhage who wanted so badly to be cured that she came up behind Jesus and touched him. Jesus responded to the touch by exclaiming, "Someone touched me; I know that power has gone forth from me" (Luke 8:46). The woman's touch had profoundly affected Jesus. Even the parables include instances of individuals expressing love and compassion through touch. In the parable of the Good Samaritan, the Samaritan cares for the suffering man through touch, by bandaging his wounds, pouring oil on them and physically bringing him to the inn. In the Parable of the Prodigal Son, the father's touch is welcoming and healing. We are told that when the wandering son returned, his father "threw his arms around his neck, and kissed him" (Luke 15:20).

Perhaps the most profound story in the Gospels in which the sense of touch is featured is that of Thomas. When we reflect on the story of doubting Thomas, or hear someone preach about it, we usually consider it to be basically about faith. Thomas seems to have little faith and therefore needs proof that Jesus is in fact alive. But the story is also one of intimacy, of getting close to God, of touching the Lord. Thomas feels that he can affirm a weak, hidden inner faith by literally touching Jesus. When the disciples approach

Thomas and excitedly proclaim, "We have seen the Lord," it
doesn't impress him. He responds, "I will never believe it without
probing the nailprints in his hands, without putting my finger in the
nailmarks and my hand into his side" (John 20:25). While we have
no evidence that Thomas actually touched Jesus, we know that he
felt a need to do so in order to believe. We, too, sometimes need to
"touch" the Lord in order to believe. The historical Jesus is not
available to us in quite the same way in which he was to Thomas,
but we can still "touch" him in our own lives by reaching out for
another's hand or by holding someone in our arms. The result of
such a touch may be absolutely overwhelming to us. It may bring
us to a deeper faith in God and a greater intimacy with him.

Think of the great power of communicating divine love that
we hold within our physical selves. God has given us the ability
through a glance, a touch, a smile, to heal and uplift one another.
We hold within ourselves a power that is awesome and even holy.

CHAPTER 9

The Agony Of Friendship

I WAS DRIVING along Bay to Bay Boulevard in my home city of Tampa one night with a very special friend, Virginia. As we rode, we reflected together on the complexities of relationships. Being in a rather bitter state, I said to her that life would be so simple, uncomplicated and painless without relationships. Virginia's response was immediate and very firmly stated: "Yes, life would be simple, uncomplicated, painless and STERILE!" Her words had a very startling ring of truth to them.

Relationships are often charged with pain. They try us, confuse us, frighten us, threaten us and make us weary — but they also uplift us and fulfill us. It is through the pain we suffer in our relationships that we strengthen our love for one another and grow as individuals. True friendships are always grace-filled even in (sometimes especially in) their darkest moments. It means that God uses these moments to speak to us of the durability of love and the reality of its issuing from the heart of Jesus.

Suffering purifies, refines and strengthens people. There is a great passage in the Old Testament that addresses reasons for affliction:

> . . . we should be grateful to the Lord our God, for putting us to the test, as he did our forefathers. Recall how he dealt with Abraham, and how he tried Isaac and all that happened to Jacob in Syrian Mesopotamia while he was tending the flock of Laban, his mother's brother. Not for vengeance did the Lord put them in the crucible to try their hearts, nor has he done so with us. It is by way of admonition that he chastises those who are close to him (Judith 8:25 – 27).

As lovers we are made tender through pain, and in tenderness we are for one another sacraments of God's love. In a relationship the true meaning of words, promises and symbols is learned in the midst of affliction. Real loving is never easy; we know from Jesus' experience that radical love leads to the cross. To live a life charged with passion is necessarily to experience suffering. The word ''passion'' comes from the Latin ''passio'' which means ''the suffering of life.'' A passionate person loves intensely and so chooses to suffer.

Passionate persons who believe in the Paschal Mystery understand that through pain there is growth, that in dying there is new life. God is revealed in a special way in a friendship when the Paschal Mystery is operative in it: when some things formerly clung to are painfully shed, uprooted and shaken so that purification and transformation can happen.

At some point in my life, I realized how much the Paschal Mystery had been operative in my friendships. I also realized that my belief in a Paschal Savior is absolutely what has sustained me in my life's sufferings. While I do not enjoy or look forward to the pain that often accompanies friendship, I am grateful for the strength to endure it, resting in the hope that from pain comes growth and new life. I pity those who do not know the wonder of the Paschal Mystery in their hearts. Their darkness must seem endless, meaningless and without purpose.

God intends the Paschal Mystery to be a part of the rhythm of our lives. Through it we come into vital contact with God's plan for our growth and for our journey toward him in intimacy. We can teach one another about the reality of the Paschal Mystery by the way we live our lives. My friends have done so by encouraging me to face my pain, to suffer well! I listen to them because I know that they will stay with me as I suffer, to comfort and encourage me.

By dying time and again, we become the kind of lovers who incarnate God for others. It is as though the pain carves a place in our hearts where God resides and shines forth, touching others through us.

To think of friendship and love in terms of suffering is not a cynical approach but a realistic one. True love must be cleansed of its sentimentality; true love is piercing and tough and requires all that we have and the best of who we are. A relationship is something we work at; something we must reflect on, value and sometimes endure outrageous pain to protect or to strengthen.

There is a wholesome brand of pain in true friendships. It is often the pain of loving too much; of knowing and experiencing that love is both tough and beautiful; of not being understood; of watching another suffer. The pain of friendship may be the pain of growing alienation or of definitive separation. Part of the pain of friendship is the conflict that often exists between two persons. This can be very healthy. When two people relate without ever conflicting, perhaps deliberately avoiding it, it is questionable whether the relationship is indeed a genuine friendship. Without glorifying conflict, it is important to note that conflict in a relationship can point to a much deeper reality. If the two people enter into a friendship fully, each encounters the other as a whole person with a multiplicity of feelings, convictions, strengths and weaknesses. In an intense relationship, inevitably in all the day to day encounters each will "bump into" the other at times. True friendships are necessarily free and liberating. Where there is disagreement in a friendship, the individuals feel free to express the conflict, to let it be. Martin Marty, in an interesting little book entitled *Friendship*, comments precisely on this idea:

> Being friends and never coming into conflict is probably a sign of apathy; people who care deeply about anything in the world are going to disagree and, if they are free, to express their disagreement. [1]

Often it is precisely through conflict that we begin to realize that God is operative in a relationship. Through all the stress and struggle of the conflict, we may see God's hand upholding both of us and even keeping the relationship together. At a time when I came into an extremely painful conflict with someone I loved deeply, I can remember that there was an underpinning of security and peace. It was as though I knew that this suffering was a necessary process that we both had to endure in order to refine and strengthen our relationship. I also knew that in the end, whatever the outcome, I could accept it because I was secure in the fact that God would allow love to triumph — and as long as love was the victor, all would be well.

Our relationship survived the conflict and is stronger and better for it. I would never ask for conflict in this or any other relationship again; the pain was far too great. But in retrospect, I thank God for it; for the grace of perseverance and especially for the insights, the growth and the strengthening of the relationship that resulted from the conflict.

In a friendship we cannot force growth or happiness or understanding. We can only remain faithful in the midst of the darkness and deeply trust that the God of life and love will bring light and strength.

Anyone who has ever been involved in a true, intense friendship knows that it involves sacrifice. One of the greatest sufferings that must be endured in a relationship is the pain of sacrifice. There is the sacrifice of ourselves, our time, our energies, our resources. In a friendship there is the sacrifice of not thinking of oneself first; of not having the last word; of allowing another to shine as we step back; of changing so as to be a better friend. The word "sacrifice" has its root in the Latin "sacrum facere" which means "to make sacred." We make something sacred by offering it to God. Jesus' sacrifice of himself made life itself sacred. If we do indeed sacrifice for the sake of our friendships, we make them sacred. A friendship between two people who have sacrificed themselves and have borne the pain of suffering together is a holy union. Because it is holy, God himself dwells within it.

It is a daring thing to enter into intimacy, to allow another to become a part of us. It means opening ourselves to hurt, making the choice to be vulnerable. Eugene Kennedy states in his book *On Being A Friend* that "the risk of living with the possibility of psychological injury at the hands of friends is inseparable from the experience we call friendship."[2] Risk is a necessary part of friendship. The deeper the intimacy, the greater the risk since there is a greater investment of self. The risk involved in friendship requires that we be open to whatever the relationship brings, that we relinquish control, that we have limitless trust. Our posture must be like that of Susanna in the Old Testament: "through her tears, she looked up to heaven, for she trusted in the Lord wholeheartedly" (Daniel 13:35).

There are those whose fear is so great that they will always sit on the sidelines of relationships. Not to act because of the fear involved in taking a risk, is to refuse to live. In his book *The Four Loves*, C.S. Lewis presents a unique commentary, laced with a bit of sarcasm, about how to avoid being hurt in a relationship:

To love at all is to be vulnerable. Love anything and your heart
will certainly be wrung and possibly broken. If we want to make
sure of keeping it intact, you must give your heart to no one, not
even an animal. Wrap it carefully around with hobbies and little
luxuries; avoid all entanglements; lock it up safe in the casket or
coffin of your selfishness. But in that casket — safe, dark,
motionless, airless — it will change. It will not be broken; it will
become unbreakable, impenetrable, irredeemable.[3]

When we enter into deep interpersonal relationships, we leave
the safety and security of the enclosed environment Lewis speaks
of. We enter into a PROMISE with all its accompanying in-
securities. When we operate within the context of a promise we are
always vulnerable. Like Abraham we leave behind all supports and
cling to the promise, trusting God unreservedly along the way. If
the promise is built on a covenant of love, we will never lose. We
may experience outrageous pain and even death, but in the end love
will triumph.

Separations are often the most painful aspect of a relationship.
The rhythm of friendship involves the dynamics of embracing and
letting go. We always seem to be coming together and parting. Life
is filled with hellos and good-byes, meetings and partings. We
have all experienced the unspeakable tragedy of separating
ourselves from those we love and the overwhelming joy of reunion.

Separations have a significant impact on our growth as
persons. Sometimes we are able to love better if we are separated
from those we love for a time. Jesus wanted his disciples to know
him more intimately when he said, ''It is much better for you that I
go. If I fail to go, the Paraclete will never come to you'' (John
16:7). There are times when our friends and family must go so that
the Spirit will come to enlighten our dark corners, to purify us and
to transform us into more perfect lovers.

Those whom we love become part of us. If we fully enter into
relationships with others, we also give away a part of ourselves, a

part which we can never retrieve. When those we love leave or die, they take a part of us with them. Much of our pain is that of grieving over the part of us that has died. But in that dying, there is transformation; a part of us dies so that we can be born anew.

The story of Abraham's near sacrifice of Isaac has always hit home for me in a very real way. It speaks to me of the sacrifices that are both a part of our relationships as well as a key to our growth in holiness. First consider what Abraham's elation must have been like in receiving the gift of a son when, according to Scripture, Sarah was beyond childbearing. So great was Abraham's joy that "on the day of the child's weaning, Abraham held a great feast" (Genesis 21:8). Then comes the test. God asks Abraham to give Isaac back. Abraham is a good man who loves God. Ironically, his love for God has grown because of the gift of Isaac. God asks Abraham for the very sacrament of his love that has helped Abraham to grow in holiness. Abraham, being a man of tremendous faith, proceeds to do what God asks. We cannot begin to imagine the anguish in Abraham's heart as he ascends the mountain with Isaac. But Isaac is spared.

Isaac does not die on Mt. Moriah, but something in Abraham dies. Abraham comes away transformed. His willingness to sacrifice Isaac, and the accompanying anguish he endures, purify him. There is no human, physical sacrifice on Mt. Moriah, but there is a sacrifice of the heart. In saying "yes" to the sacrificing of his son, Abraham expresses a willingness to sacrifice his own heart. He agreed to wrench Isaac from the depths of his heart and give him back to God. It is not an easy thing to do, but Abraham believes in a God of life and so trusts God with all his heart. In this sacrifice, Abraham sanctified his life, Isaac's life and all of life. His relationship with Isaac becomes even more sacred, firmly rooted in the life-giving God. Actually, Abraham does not fully get Isaac back. Because Abraham descends Mt. Moriah changed, he realizes that while Isaac was a gift from God, he was not meant for Abraham to possess or hoard.

God has given me several Isaacs, those wonderful people who have entered my life at times when I never expected them and brought me great joy. God has also asked me to give up several of my Isaacs. My willingness to do this never seems to measure up to Abraham's. It is as though, unlike Abraham, I ascend my Mt. Moriah cursing and complaining and pleading with God to change his mind. Somehow, though, I know that such separation is a way of growing in holiness. However relunctantly, I allow them to go, clinging to the promise that the Spirit will come.

There is a certain bond among those who have borne pain. Pain draws us to one another, especially when it is a common pain. In this union of pain, often we discover the ever-present God. It happens at Alcoholics Anonymous, it happens in groups of divorcees, widows, widowers, etc. In friendship we share our brokenness. No one can come into intimacy with another without sharing that person's suffering. In this intimacy of the weak, the suffering and the grieving, love is born. True love comes only from God, and he is a felt presence among those who are not only broken but who also share in the intimacy of pain with others.

The closer we get to God, the more intense are the demands made upon us. There is a brief line in the Old Testament that really bothers me: "Give me your heart" (Proverbs 23:26). God asks nothing less of us than our very hearts. Of course, giving your heart can be very painful and difficult. *Hinds Feet on High Places* is a magnificent little book by Hannah Hurnard. It is an allegory about a young girl whose name is Much Afraid. The deepest desire of her heart is to be united to God in intimacy. Allegorically, this is expressed in terms of acquiring hind's feet. For Much Afraid, to have hind's feet and the ability to get to the High Places means to follow the path the Shepherd has mapped out for her. In response to Much Afraid's request to go to the High Places, the Shepherd tells her that "no one is allowed to dwell in the Kingdom of Love, unless they have the flower of Love already blooming in their

hearts.''⁴   Much Afraid wants nothing else but to have love
planted in her heart, so the Shepherd begins the process:

> The Shepherd put His hand in His bosom, drew something forth,
> and laid it in the palm of His hand. Then he held His hand out
> toward Much Afraid. 'Here is the seed of Love,' He said.
>
> She bent forward to look, then gave a startled little cry and drew
> back. There was indeed a seed lying in the palm of His hand, but
> it was shaped exactly like a long, sharply pointed thorn.
>
> 'This seed looks very sharp,' she said shrinkingly.
> 'Won't it hurt if you put it into my heart?'
>
> He answered gently, 'It is so sharp that it slips in very quickly.
> But, Much Afraid, I have already warned you that Love and Pain
> go together, for a time at least. If you would know Love, you
> must know pain too.'

Much afraid agreed to have the thorn planted in her heart and
many times on the journey to the High Places the thorn made her
pierced heart throb and ache. When she arrived at the High Places,
the Shepherd asked her to open her heart so that He could see what
was there:

> At His word she laid bare her heart, and out came the sweetest
> perfume she had ever breathed and filled all the air around them
> with the fragrance. There in her heart was a plant whose shape
> and form could not be seen because it was covered all over with
> pure white, almost transparent blooms, from which the fra-
> grance poured forth.⁵

The thorn-shaped seed had blossomed into magnificent
flowers. Much Afraid surrendered her heart to the Shepherd and

allowed pain to engulf it, but her pain was transformed into incomparable joy.

There is a lesson for us in this allegory. For us to lay bare our hearts to God and allow him to plant a thorn there is to open ourselves to human love with all its agonies and ecstasies. It is to make ourselves vulnerable by giving others power over us, power to even hurt us. Like Much Afraid, we trust the Shepherd enough that we cling to his promise that the thorn-like seeds in our lives will burst forth into the loveliest, most fragrant blossoms. We must be willing to pay the tremendous price of the giving of our very hearts in love to one another, trusting God every step of the way. If we do this, we will not only experience the joy of human intimacy, but also intimacy with the God of love himself.

Friendship can be an experience of ecstasy, but it will always carry with it the anguish of deep suffering. Amid the joy and pain, there is always something mysteriously good and irresistible about it. It is something that hints of the magnificence of an all-loving God.

CHAPTER 10

Where Friendship Leads

INTERESTINGLY, when two people meet at a level of deep personal love sustained by intimacy, commitment, affirmation and trust, they do not merge with each other so as to lose their individual identities. Instead, they find themselves and thus find new freedom.

Liberation is the experience by which we realize in a deeply personal way that we are loved and accepted just as we are. We are liberated through gracious love. Such love does not require that we do anything to deserve it. That's what happened when Jesus expressed his overwhelming love for us on the cross. It is what happens when the gracious love of God is shared through the channels of human hearts.

In an earlier chapter, I discussed the power of grace. Grace or God's gracious love not only has the power to save and transform us, but it also liberates us to be wholly ourselves and to give ourselves wholly to God and to one another. One of the greatest things we can do for others is to allow them to be themselves. With the freedom to be ourselves comes interior peace even when there is external turmoil in life. Whenever we feel free in a relationship, we need not weigh our words or worry about the impressions we make on the other. To be with a true friend is to be "at home." I have mentioned earlier that part of the appeal of the movie "E.T." was that it spoke to us of our need for another's presence. More specifically, it touched our yearning to "be at home." The Extra-Terrestrial expressed the single-hearted desire to GO HOME throughout the film. All of us yearn to go "home" where we can BE at home. "Home" is not necessarily a geographic place or building. Home is where we are most ourselves, where we can be ourselves without pretenses and with total comfort. Home is literally and figuratively where we can take off our shoes and put our feet on the furniture. We loved E.T. because, like us, he wanted the freedom of being at home. When we are loved just as we are, we are liberated and we find that we are at home.

Our friends are those persons who say to us, "It's okay to be you." In *Friendship in the Lord*, Paul Hinnebusch, O.P. has this to say about the liberating power of friendship:

> For until I have experienced loving friendship, subconsciously I am constantly worried about myself, fearing that I am nothing, nothing worthy of love and attention.[1]

Jesus' encounter with Zacchaeus says something to us about the liberating nature of friendship. Zacchaeus is liberated because Jesus dared to call him forth and to unabashedly express his love for him. Zacchaeus knew from the heart that he was lovable because Jesus loved him. Zacchaeus was free to be himself after that encounter, because Jesus' love affirmed him to be the person God intended him to be.

No one can possibly find true liberation within impersonal situations and alienating structures. True liberation comes through the realization of being loved. Only love is redemptive, because God IS love and only he can redeem us. Jesus is our Redeemer because he is the total embodiment of the absolute love of God for us. That same absolute love of God continues to be embodied in all those who love genuinely from the heart.

The genuine, freeing love of another is a sure sign in our lives of the presence and love of God. God's unconditional love tells us that we are totally free to be who we are; that despite our sinfulness we will never be deprived of God's love. God's love is redemptive love; it is the only true love that exists. Therefore, relationships in which true love is shared are indeed redemptive.

We are our truest selves before God because he knows us through and through. As Psalm 139 so beautifully puts it:

> O Lord, you probed me and you know
> me;
> you know when I sit and when I
> stand;
> you understand my thoughts from
> afar.
> My journeys and my rest you
> scrutinize,
> with all my ways you are familiar.
> Even before a word is on my tongue,
> behold, O Lord, you know the whole of
> it (Psalm 139:1-4).

The truly wondrous thing about all that this Psalm expresses is that God knows us totally — our talents, our faults and short-comings — and he still loves us. This complete acceptance by God is hard to believe. We are not accustomed to total acceptance. Those persons in our lives who set us free by affirming us provide us with a sure glimpse of God's total acceptance. They make God's overwhelming love believable for us here and now.

With this liberation there is an uplifting of the spirit and a very definite joy. Meeting God in another human being brings us the purest kind of joy. A true sense of joy is always rooted in God, and he makes us messengers of it for one another. We need people of joy in our lives, people of the resurrection like Mary Magdalene, who have seen the Lord and are willing to share the joy of that encounter.

In a genuine friendship there is a mysterious sense that something good and enriching is happening to us, that we are moving closer to God. With this sense comes a mysterious joy grounded in the awareness that we are full of possibilities as individuals and that together we are capable of magnificent miracles. Some researchers hold that people who are involved in deep friendship or who are in love actually experience increased energy levels. In essence, love penetrates us with an energizing force — with the joy of God.

When we truly "know" God, something happens in us. Even though it happens from within, it shows outwardly. There is a quiet, tender joy about a person who has consciously touched God. It is a joy that is meant to be shared; there is even an urgency in us to share it. In the Eucharistic community, we gather specifically to share our joy in the Lord, which he has allowed us to experience individually and as a community.

There is a marked difference between pleasure and joy. Pleasure is easy to find, and is usually momentary; but joy comes through struggle and pain, and it lasts. Too often we spend our time and energy seeking pleasure, thinking that it will mend us in broken places and ultimately bring fulfillment. Soon we find that there is only momentary relief. True joy, on the contrary, touches the very core of our being because it always originates in God. We have the privilege of experiencing the very joy of God through one another.

The most joyful moments in my life have been those when I have sensed the presence of God in a very real way through some human situations. In these instances, I have found myself spontaneously praising God for his graciousness in being present to me in ways I would have never expected. Most often these have been times of intimate sharing with a friend. In our sharing there was a peace and joy beyond our comprehension. It was a quiet "high" charged with meaning. The joy that is God's special gift to us is like that. It doesn't jar us into elation. Instead, there is a quiet and peace that lulls us into the experience of a special brand of joy, the joy that only God can provide. Our union with one another serves as a channel for that joy.

Friendships that channel such joy into our lives must themselves be joyful. Friendships in which individuals have fun, in which laughter, joking and teasing season the relationship provide us with a taste of the lasting joy of the Lord. If a friendship is genuine and based on deep and lasting commitment, there is always joy. We rejoice in one another. We rejoice in the fact that the other exists. That is why we celebrate the birthdays of those whom we love. We celebrate because they were born and came to be a part of our lives. We celebrate their existence and how it has played a significant and even vital role in our search for life's deepest meaning. We rejoice in the Lord, recognizing that something so wholesome and uplifting can only be rooted in a God who is gracious enough to give us to one another.

The supreme joy will come from ultimate, total union with God. Here and now our journey toward that ultimate union is studded with the ongoing experience of relating to one another in our human situations. Life will try us and pull us down into the pits of darkness where pain and sorrow permeate us, but we know the promise of joy. It is written on our hearts. Amid the tears we cling to that promise as we cling to one another. Jesus made the promise clear:

I tell you truly:
you will weep and mourn while
the world rejoices;
You will grieve for a time,
but your grief will be turned
into joy (John 16:20).

CHAPTER 11

We Long To See
The Face Of God

A PROMINENT THEME in the Psalms
is a deep longing for God. For example, Psalm 42 reflects the
Psalmist's ardent desire for God:

> As the hind longs for running waters,
> so my soul longs for you, O God.
> Athirst is my soul for God, the living God.
> When shall I go and behold the face of God?
> (Psalm 42:2-3).

Using vivid images, Psalm 63 speaks of the same longing and
the ultimate, total satisfaction that comes only from God:

> O God, you are my God whom I seek;
> for you my flesh pines and my soul thirsts
> like the earth, parched, lifeless and without water
> (Psalm 63:2).

Psalm 130, often used at funeral liturgies, beautifully expresses a profound yearning for union with God:

> I trust in the Lord;
> My soul trusts in his word.
> My soul waits for the Lord
> more than sentinels wait for the dawn
> (Psalm 130:5-6).

Also, time and again the classic spiritual writers express a longing for God. Often this longing is at the center of their spirituality. It is evident in John of the Cross, Teresa of Avila, Catherine of Siena and Augustine, to mention but a few. They express the truth that our experience of God is synonymous with a deep longing for more from life, and with a basic restlessness with life.

The heart of every person is ontologically oriented toward God. In her moving *Revelations of Divine Love*, Juliana of Norwich has this to say about our ultimate desire for union with God:

> Our natural will is to have God, and the good will of God is to have us, and we may never cease willing or longing for him until we have him in the fullness of joy, and then we shall be no longer. [1]

In another chapter she makes the point that until we rest in God, we will never experience fulfillment:

> But I cannot tell the reality of him who is my maker, lover and keeper, for until I am united to him in substance, I may never have the complete rest or real bliss, that is, until I am so fastened to him that there is absolutely no created thing between my God and me. [2]

And again in Chapter 26, Juliana speaks of this longing for God:

> . . . our soul shall never have rest until it comes to him, knowing that he is the fullness of joy, familiarly and courteously blissful, and life itself.[3]

Put simply, true fulfillment in life comes through ultimate union with God. All human intimacy is an approximation of that fulfillment, but no human relationship does it all for us. We learn through the ultimate incompleteness of every human relationship that there is total fulfillment only in something that is yet to come; that our ultimate connection is to God.

In human intimacy there is a taste of fulfillment and a longing for more. At the center of each person there is a longing heart that can only be satisfied in intimacy with God. In our intimacy with one another, our longing for God intensifies. Every ''fulfillment'' in a relationship is actually only a partial fulfillment of the ultimate. Human intimacy helps us to sense that there is something more, something even greater than the ecstasy of such a relationship. It is for this that we secretly and deeply yearn.

Once we experience the ecstasy of human intimacy, we simultaneously experience some frustration in that the fulfillment falls somewhat short. It is but a taste, a glimpse of the fullness that is only possible through intimacy with God.

In faith-filled relationships based on genuine love, we know that the best is yet to come. Again, Ladislaus Boros puts it well:

> To be seized by the absolute that shines through the friend, to be carried up by it into the boundless and to realize at the same time that the other person whose being we so totally affirm is still not fulfillment: this is the great sadness, but also the happiness of friendship. To sense the infinite in the finite, this is the nature of friendship.[4]

All of us need someone who fully knows us and loves us. We have the feeling that this someone exists. Actually, life fully lived is a journey toward, a relentless search for, and ultimately a clinging to that Someone.

Early in a personal spiritual journey, I came to a deep realization and boldly announced to my spiritual director, "I want intimacy with God!" Somehow I knew that this was the bottom line. It is all that really matters, and we must spend our lives in pursuit of intimacy with the divine. We are made for communion with God; that is our destiny. In my own spiritual journey, I have come to realize that there is a part of me that cannot be contained in words, definitions, ideologies or beliefs and certainly not in institutions. It is a part of me that is uplifted but never satisfied in human intimacies. It is a part of me that is limitless and bound only for God.

An understanding of this longing for the ultimate satisfaction that comes only from union with God is particularly bound up with our human intimacies. Often in the midst of a profound experience of beauty we are reminded and brought closer to the glory of the Creator. When we experience the profound beauty of another person and the magic of human love, we are drawn to the ultimate magnificence of the God of love. But at the same time we know the experience in all its beauty to be only a faint reflection of the ecstasy of divine intimacy.

All love is bound up with God. Our human loves remind us of God and lead us to him. Even their incompleteness brings us to a deeper understanding that our greatest longing is for God. Martin Helldorfer has this to say on this point:

> All human relationships, particularly those of love, leave us
> standing alone in a way that points to the one relationship for
> which we hunger and toward which we move. Love, intimate
> human love — its presence as well as its absence — awakens and

reawakens the sense that we are participating in a mystery far
beyond our comprehension and that God continues to beckon us
in the most human of ways.[5]

God gives us one another, the ability to love, the sense of
being uplifted in love, and the warmth and beauty of human
friendship so that we will ultimately be drawn to him. Basically,
we are made for him.

In human love we not only experience a longing for the total
fulfillment that comes only in union with God, but we also
recognize common longing in each other. In a wonderful and
profound friendship at one point in my life, my friend and I knew
that the basis of our oneness did not lie in common interests or
mutual attraction but in a common SOURCE, the One in whom
both of us "live and move and have our being" (Acts 17:28), the
One for whom both of us longed.

I cannot imagine a genuine human friendship where true love
flourishes that is not grounded in a shared dream of the Kingdom, a
joint longing for the One who makes all our dreams come true.

All our interpersonal relationships bring special depth and
meaning to our lives, but never will they bring that completeness
for which we all long. We will forever remain unfulfilled until God
brings to fruition the final love affair. All that we experience in our
human loves is not enough. That is why there is an eternity when
we will meet the ultimate Lover face to face.

We are indeed born hungry. While many may never come to
name that for which they hunger, basically all of us hunger for
God. Nothing less than an intimate relationship with him will
satisfy us. Our human relationships bring the God of our longings
into better focus. If we are attentive to the urging of the Spirit
within us and among us, our relationships will ultimately bring us
to Christ himself. In a wonderfully uplifting passage, Aelred of
Rievaulx views human intimacy as a way to intimacy with Christ:

So when all earthly affections have been mastered and when all
earthly desires have been lulled to sleep, the mind finds delight
in the kiss of only Christ, rests in his embrace, exulting and
saying: 'His left hand is under my head; his right hand shall
embrace me.'[6]

Our human friendships can be beautiful, uplifting and holy.
They can also be frightening, painful and distressing. But if seen
within the context of God's plan for us and his own desire for
intimacy with us, our human loves point to the one divine love, the
only totally satisfying love. As John of the Cross put it:

> For the sickness of love is not cured except by
> Your very presence and image.[7]

Conclusion

Too OFTEN WE LOOK for sensa-
tional signs of God's love when all we have to do is look to the
person next to us. To some degree God means for us to answer each
other's prayers so as to bring each other into the realm of the sacred
and there find the only true, lasting fulfillment.

We were born to be lovers. God intended for us to fall in love
with one another. We are our best selves when we love because in
loving we enter into the ultimate experience, that of God himself.
What a magnificent God it is who uses something as wonderful as
friendship to reveal himself to us!

Our human loves are inexorably bound up with divine love.
They often lead to God. Our journeys toward one another in
genuine friendship end only in eternity; true friendship is always
evolving and growing toward God.

Ladislaus Boros commented that "Heaven, the essentiality of
being, where everything achieves its full authenticity, is already
close to us in friendship."[1]   Friendship can indeed be a glimpse
of the eternal for us.

[95]

We are especially and wonderfully graced if we have intimate friends who are deeply aware of their communion with God, consciously filled with his Holy Spirit and disposed to sharing their experience of the living God. With such persons, in holy relationship, there is a mutual participation in God's convenantal love.

Perhaps the worst thing that could ever happen to us is that we become closed to the offerings of love around us:

> Oh, that today you would hear his voice:
> Harden not your hearts . . . (Psalm 96:7-8)

We "hear" the voice of God whenever we experience the warmth and wonder of the love of another human person.

Certainly, I cannot *prove* anything I have said in this little book. The only "proof" that readers may discover can be found by responding to an invitation to relate in love to another human being and therein come to intimately know the God who is love.

Those genuine friendships, grounded in the love of God, that I have experienced and continue to experience have illuminated life for me. They have brought me to touch the face of God himself. All genuine human love relationships are tied into a Center — the center of all life and love — the heart of Jesus Christ.

Endnotes

CHAPTER 1

1 William McNamara, *Earthly Mysticism* (New York: Crossroad, 1983), p. 2.
2 Gerald O'Mahony, *Abba! Father! A Personal Catechism* (New York: Crossroad, 1982), p. 73.
3 Ladislaus Boros, *Meeting God in Man* (Garden City, New York: Doubleday, 1968), p. 115.
4 Donald Nicholl, *Holiness* (New York: Seabury Press, 1981), p. 116.
5 Abraham Heschel, *I Asked for Wonder* (New York: Crossroad, 1984), p. 99.
6 Nicholl, p. 117.
7 Sam Keen, *The Passionate Life* (San Francisco: Harper and Row, 1983), p. 251.
8 Saint Augustine, *The Soliloquies of Saint Augustine*, trans. by Thomas F. Gilligan (New York: Cosmopolitan Science and Art Service Co., Inc., 1943). I, 7.
9 C.S. Lewis, *The Four Loves* (New York: Harcourt Brace Jovanovich, 1960), p. 126.

CHAPTER 2

1 Aelred of Rievaulx, *Spiritual Friendship* (Kalamazoo, Michigan: Cistercian Publications, 1974), p. 73.
2 Saint Francis de Sales, *Introduction to the Devout Life*, trans. and ed. by John K. Ryan (Garden City, New York: Doubleday, 1966), p. 175.
3 Gary Inrig, *Quality Friendship* (Chicago: Moody Press, 1981), p. 152.
4 John Powell, *Unconditional Love* (Niles, Illinois: Argus Communications, 1978), p. 68.
5 Morton T. Kelsey, *Caring* (New York: Paulist Press, 1981), p. 21.
6 Charles A. Gallagher, George A. Maloney, Mary F. Rousseau, and Paul F. Wilczak, *Embodied in Love* (New York: Crossroad, 1983), p. 31.
7 Richard P. McBrien, *Catholicism* (Minneapolis, Minnesota: Winston Press, 1980), p. 182.

8 Evelyn Eaton Whitehead and James D. Whitehead, *Christian Life Patterns* (Garden City, New York: Doubleday, 1979), p. 77.
9 Morton T. Kelsey, *Companions on the Inner Way* (New York: Crossroad, 1983), p. 198.

CHAPTER 3

1 Morris West, *The Clowns of God* (New York: William Morrow and Co., Inc., 1981), pp. 203-204.
2 William Johnston, *Silent Music* (New York: Harper and Row, 1974), p. 141.
3 Saint Augustine, *The Confessions of Saint Augustine*, trans. by John K. Ryan (Garden City, New York: Image Books, 1960), p. 43.

CHAPTER 5

1 William McNamara, *Mystical Passion* (New York: Paulist Press, 1977), p. 123.

CHAPTER 6

1 John Powell, *Unconditional Love* (Niles, Illinois: Argus Communications, 1978), p. 56.
2 Bernard J. Bush, *Living In His Love* (Whitinsville, Massachusetts: Affirmation Books, 1978), p. 103.
3 Ladislaus Boros, *Meeting God In Man* (Garden City, New York: Doubleday, 1968), p. 74.
4 M. Scott Peck, *The Road Less Travelled* (New York: Simon and Schuster, 1978), p. 153.

CHAPTER 8

1 Matthew Fox, *Whee! We, wee All the Way Home* . . . (Santa Fe, New Mexico: Bear and Company, Inc., 1981), p. 186.

CHAPTER 9

1 Martin E. Marty, *Friendship* (Allen, Texas: Argus Communications, 1980), p. 197.
2 Eugene Kennedy, *On Being A Friend* (New York: The Continuum Publishing Company, 1982), p. 48.
3 C.S. Lewis, *The Four Loves* (New York: Harcourt Brace Jovanovich, 1960), p. 169.

4 Hannah Hurnard, *Hind's Feet On High Places* (Wheaton, Illinois: Tyndale House Publishers, Inc., 1976), p. 17.
5 *Ibid.*, p. 199.

CHAPTER 10

1 Paul Hinnebusch, *Friendship In The Lord* (Notre Dame, Indiana: Ave Maria Press, 1974), p. 38.

CHAPTER 11

1 Juliana of Norwich, *Revelations of Divine Love*, trans, by M.L. del Mastro (Garden City, New York: Image Books, 1977), p. 92.
2 *Ibid.*, p. 88.
3 *Ibid.*, p. 123.
4 Ladislaus Boros, *Meeting God In Man* (Garden City, New York: Doubleday, 1968), p. 77.
5 Sean D. Sammon, ed., *Relationships* (Whitinsville, Massachusetts: Affirmation Books, 1983), p. 27.
6 Aelred of Rievaulx, *Spiritual Friendship* (Kalamazoo, Michigan: Cistercian Publications, 1974), p. 77.
7 Kieran Kavanaugh and Otilio Rodriguez, trans., *The Collected Works of St. John of the Cross* (Washington, D.C.: Institute of Carmelite Studies, 1979), p. 411.

CONCLUSION

1 Ladislaus Boros, *Meeting God In Man* (Garden City, New York: Doubleday, 1968) p. 76.

FEELINGS AND EMOTIONS IN CHRISTIAN LIVING
Mary Michael O'Shaughnessy, OP

Joy, grief, anger and fear are four of the principal emotions which play a central role in our affective life as Christians. They can be constructive or destructive, liberating or enslaving, life-giving or death-dealing. Sound principles of psychology and sound Scriptural theology give us guidelines and strategies for managing these emotions and our affective life in a positive and healthy way, both from a physical and a spiritual point of view. This book is concerned with the correlation and the integration of our affective behavior with the Gospel message and the affective impact of the Christ-event on us in the twentieth century. All those who are intent upon their own spiritual growth and development will find it eminently helpful.

Sister Mary Michael O'Shaughnessy, OP is nationally known for her workshops, regional conferences and national symposiums on religious education, faith development and Christian spirituality. She received her doctorate from Catholic University of America and has done post doctoral study at the University of Chicago Divinity School. She is perhaps best known for her authorship, along with Fathers Weber and Kilgallon of two complete Religious Education Programs for the elementary school child, *Word and Worship* and *The Word is Life*, both published by Benziger. More recently she co-authored with Father James Kilgallon *Becoming Catholic Even if You Happen to Be One*. This is her first book for Alba House.

0524-7   166 pages

CELIBACY, PRAYER AND FRIENDSHIP
A Making Sense-Out-of-Life Approach
Christopher Kiesling, OP

"This is not just 'another' book on celibacy. It bespeaks a seasoned author's mind. The publishers are to be congratulated for putting out such a large book at so modest a price and for making available a work so pregnant with valuable information." *Sisters Today*

". . . as a whole, this book is probably the best treatment available on the celibate life." Donald Goergen, OP, *National Catholic Reporter*

"In the welter of material on sexuality and spirituality churned out these days, it is refreshing to find a book which integrates both dimensions of life in a manner that is balanced, personal and theologically sound."
Spirituality Today

BAH068   229 pages   14,000 sold!

SO I'M NOT PERFECT:
A Psychology of Humility
Robert J. Furey, PhD

Self-acceptance is the foundation of all emotional health and spiritual growth. It is also, unfortunately, one of the most difficult hurdles we have to overcome on our way to spiritual and psychological well-being. Enter the misunderstood and often badly abused virtue of humility, a virtue closely allied with the truth which Christ proclaimed would set us free. This is, then, a book about truth and growth and the freedom to be.

Robert Furey is a counseling psychologist in St. Louis. He received his B.A. from Boston College and his M.S. and Ph.D. from St. Louis University. Dr. Furey has taught classes at St. Louis University and St. Louis Community College and has given workshops and presentations nationwide on such topics as human development and bereavement. He is a member of The American Psychological Association and The American Association for Counseling and Development. This is his first book.

0499-2   131 pages